NAIKAN

NAIKAN

Gratitude, Grace, and
the Japanese Art of Self-Reflection

Gregg Krech

Stone Bridge Press • *Berkeley, California*

Published by
STONE BRIDGE PRESS
P. O. Box 8208, Berkeley, CA 94707
TEL 510-524-8732 • sbp@stonebridge.com • www.stonebridge.com

10 9 8 7 6 5 4 3 2 1

2006 2005 2004 2003 2002

LIBRARY OF CONGRESS CATALOGING-IN-PUBLICATION DATA
Krech, Gregg.
    Naikan: gratitude, grace, and the Japanese art of self-reflection /
Gregg Krech.
        p. cm.
    Includes bibliographical references and index.
    ISBN 1-880656-63-9
    1. Naikan psychotherapy. I. Title.

    RC489.M43 K743 2001
    616.89'14—dc21

                                        2001054927

> **"The unexamined life is
> not worth living."**
> SOCRATES

Dedicated to my parents, Ted and Michelle, who brought me into this world from nothingness, and to my teachers, Rev. Kenryu Tsuji, Rev. Shue Usami, Kinuko Yoshimoto, Akira Ishii Sensei, Masahiro Nagashima Sensei, and David K. Reynolds, who escort me on the return trip.

Contents

Preface

In 1991 a movie was released called *Defending Your Life* and starring Albert Brooks and Meryl Streep. The story line centered around several characters who died and were transported to a temporary location where a decision was made about their future. The purpose of this place—which was a rather comfortable, almost resort-like city—was to give people who passed through a chance to watch film highlights of their lives. They had a chance to defend their conduct and the choices they made while alive, and subsequently a final decision was made about their future. They might be sent back to earth to "try again" or, if their lives were generally laudable, they would "move on" to some higher form of existence.

What I found most interesting about the film was the idea of stepping back and observing your life. In 1989 I had the opportunity to do just that for the first time, at a center located amidst the rice paddies in rural Japan. It was a Naikan center. The word Naikan means literally *looking inside*. In the fourteen days I stayed at the center I spent about fifteen hours per day watching the films of my life run across the screen of my mind's eye. Prior to this experience I had been to dozens of retreats and spiritual conferences. I had spent at least one week each year on a solo trip in the wilderness to simply be quiet in nature. I had meditated in forests and at Zen monasteries for days and weeks at a time. Yet I had never really stepped back from my life to simply see how I had been living.

The process used at the Naikan center was very structured. I reflected on the relationships with nearly all the key people that had played an influential role in my life. In each case I looked at three aspects of that relationship: *What I had received from that person. What I had given to that person. The troubles or difficulties I had caused that person.* I sat on Japanese-style cushions and faced a blank wall in order to limit outside distractions. Except for the time it took to eat, sleep, and go to the bathroom, I did little else for two weeks. In some ways I resembled the characters in the movie I have referred to, except that I had the opportunity to do this—fortunately—while I was still alive.

During my time at the Naikan center I had doubts. Why spend time reviewing my past, when there was so much to do now? Why spend time considering the troubles I was causing others when I was already striving so hard to be a good person? Wasn't Naikan for *others* who were selfishly and blindly causing suffering to friends, family, and society? Wasn't it for people who had unresolved issues from their childhood? Wasn't it for those who had a bad attitude toward life? What was I doing here?

Notwithstanding my persistent questions and doubts, I persevered each day with the review of my personal history, as far back as I could remember. As the days passed, I began to understand what was attractive *and* uncomfortable about Naikan. Naikan involved self-examination; that is, we examine our own life, not the actions of others. How often is our attention wasted on judging, criticizing, and correcting others while we neglect the examination and lessons of our own life? While we can never know the actual experience of another, we know our own experience intimately. While we can do little or nothing to control how others treat us, we can do much to control how we treat others. And while we are often powerless to impose our choices on others, we make choices about how we shall live, moment to moment, day to day. Examining one's own life is profoundly sensible, though not necessarily comfortable.

Naikan was originally developed by a Japanese man named Ishin Yoshimoto (1916–88). It is based on an austere method of self-examination called *mishirabe* and rooted in some of the ideas and principles of Pure Land Buddhism. This form of Buddhism emphasizes faith rather than effort. And the seeds of such faith are born from an awareness of two facets of one's life: First, the limitless compassion that is bestowed upon us by life; and second, the inherent self-centeredness that permeates our actions and thoughts.

The source of this compassion is not Buddha or God (though, ultimately, it can be understood that way) but is rather the everyday efforts of others to support and care for us. Through the intense and reality-based examination of our lives, we can develop a natural and profound sense of gratitude for blessings bestowed on us by others. Blessings that were always there but went unnoticed, unappreciated. How could we live without the care of others? Life blossoms before our eyes, or rather the blossoming continues but we are now aware of it. It is the joy, appreciation, and gratitude that often attract people to Naikan. We see how much we have received from life. We see the countless ways we have been loved and cared for. Despite our failures, life has not failed us. In spite of our mistakes, reality has supported us.

A Naikan retreat can be a profound and life-changing experience for many people. It is a remarkable foundation for understanding and practicing self-reflection. But it must be complemented by a regular, ongoing practice of self-reflection, or the experience and lessons simply fade from consciousness. In this sense Naikan is similar to yoga, meditation, or prayer. The consistent practice is what fertilizes the seeds and allows them to grow.

In this book I hope to introduce you to the basic practice of Naikan self-reflection, to the ideas associated with self-reflection, the underlying issues, and the various ways of incorporating these methods and ideas into your life. I offer you a wide array of vehicles for understanding Naikan—essays, poems, fables, quotes, and actual reports (results) of personal self-reflection (mine and others). As you study this material, be cautious of the apparent simplicity of this method. Naikan seems simple, though it is certainly not easy to do. Naikan appears Japanese, though it is firmly grounded in reality and the fundamental nature of the human condition. It seems superficial, yet it is capable of stripping away layers of our selves and revealing realities previously hidden. It stimulates joy blended with guilt, faith stirred by doubt, and effort uncovered by surrender. As a method of inquiry, it is a creature of contradictions. But contradictions only exist within our minds. Reality is without contradiction.

As you read this book, I hope your innate curiosity and wisdom help you surmount the limitations of my words and lead you to actually try Naikan. In the first part of the book I have provided a series of exercises for doing this. Step back. Find a space. Quietly reflect on your life. See what can be found and what can be learned. The study of reality is a worthy pursuit. And Naikan is a method of investigation, worthy of investigation.

Acknowledgments

The task of investigating all the people, objects, and forces of nature that made this book possible could generate another book. Not only do the seeds of these ideas come from so many different sources, but the ability to gather those seeds (reading, hearing, doing) and to put them on paper (writing) requires a supporting cast, all of whom are truly coauthors of this book.

If I began chronologically, I would begin with my parents, Ted and Michelle, who gave me life. Had they done nothing else, I would be deeply indebted to them. But throughout my childhood they cared for me while I failed to provide any appreciation in return. Thank you. My first-grade teacher, Mrs. Meyers, was instrumental in helping me read. And reading has exposed me to the wisdom of some great writers. A short list might include Benjamin Franklin, Albert Schweitzer, R. H. Blyth, D. T. Suzuki, C. S. Lewis, Lewis Thomas, Bishop Fulton J. Sheen, Haya Akegarasu, La Rochefoucauld, Gyodo Haguri, O. H. Mowrer, Taitetsu Unno, Thomas Merton, and many others. As a young adult, I came across a book by author and anthropologist David K. Reynolds, and it provided me with my first introduction to Naikan. I began working with Reynolds directly, and he provided me with much of my early guidance in a world of self-reflection that was both new and challenging to me. He later made arrangements for me to study Naikan in Japan with experienced teachers. He is a teacher who demands much of his students and has an extraordinary dedication to his work. My job, my writing, and my family can all be traced back to the crossing of our paths. Thank you, David.

During my trips to Japan, I had the good fortune of experiencing Naikan self-reflection at different Naikan centers under the guidance of excellent teachers whose lives often were an example of the beauty of this art of self-reflection. These teachers include Rev. Shue Usami, Akira Ishii, Masahiro Nagashima, Yoshihiko Miki, and Mrs. Yoshimoto, the wife of the founder of Naikan reflection, Ishin Yoshimoto. I vividly remember the extraordinary gentleness and softness of Mrs. Yoshimoto's eyes when I would meet with her and share my Naikan reflection from my past. She and her husband worked tirelessly for half a century to introduce this practice to the world. Thank you.

My interest in Naikan may never have been there without the stimulation and teachings of Kenryu T. Tsuji, a Pure Land Buddhist priest who spent more than ten years teaching me about Shin Buddhism. And my special thanks to Zen master Thich Nhat Hanh for showing me the gentle side of Zen and teaching me to smile while meditating.

My colleagues have been instrumental in encouraging my study of Naikan. I am especially grateful to Sue Cole, Jiun Tarasewicz, Gregory Willms, Perri Ardman, Ron and Cindy Green, Barbara Sarah, Hal Lier, Marilyn Murray, and others who have worked alongside me during the past twelve years of Naikan retreats and workshops. What a wonderful gift it has been to know and work with such lovely people.

During the years of writing this book, I had the constant companionship and devotion of my dog, Rocky. He would curl up next to my desk and give me the pleasure of stroking his soft, black fur in between paragraphs. His insistence on taking me for walks helped keep my body healthy and gave me time to reflect on what I was writing. I miss you, Rocky. Thank you. I was lucky to find Peter Goodman of Stone Bridge Press, whose personal interest in Naikan made our partnership a blessing, and I thank Perri Ardman, my good friend and colleague, for introducing Peter to the manuscript of this book and to me. And I would like to thank Michael Ashby for doing such a fine job copyediting this book. His mastery of the English and Japanese languages has done much to improve the readability of the pages that follow.

Through the years of writing and rewriting the manuscript, I have had the gift of a full-time teacher, editor, proofreader, colleague, and companion all rolled up into one amazing person—my wife, Linda. She does an admirable job of living what I write about. She embraces the idea that a relationship is a vehicle for training, and I am thankful to have such a dedicated partner.

Finally I hope that each of my readers will take a moment to remember and thank all of the beings behind the scenes who made this book appear before them—the printer who runs the press that printed these pages, the truck driver who delivered this book to the store, the trees whose bodies were sacrificed to make these pages, the person who typeset the words, and the person who took time to put the book on a shelf somewhere so it could be discovered and read. And please remember the people who taught you to read. And perhaps those who manufactured your glasses or contact lenses as well. As we follow the complex web of connections between one heart and another, we may discover the true nature of this extraordinary universe, and in doing so, we may come to rejoice in who we are and in the gift of life.

Thank you.

G. K.

Introduction

Sometimes I go out in the woods and just sit. Then I become aware of how noisy it is. Most of that noise comes from inside my head. It's filled with ideas and plans. There appears to be an endless stream of thoughts, complaints, fears, worries, hopes, and dialogue. A to-do list pops up regularly. "Don't forget to check the oil in the car." "Remember to return the library books." I'm generally not aware of this noise. My life is too busy. It's so busy that even when my body stops, my mind doesn't. My mind seems to roll on from momentum. For a while.

After a while it begins to quiet down. Then I start to hear real noise, noise from the world around me. The sounds of the chickadees talking to each other. The screech of a blue jay overhead. The clicking of a flitting hummingbird defending its territory. I notice the blossoms of a new columbine and the emptied acorn shells piled next to a rugged oak. Such sounds and sights are music. They are real. They are happening right now.

As I listen to the conversation of a red squirrel in the maple tree across from me, I notice how the rest of the music fades into the background. Even the maple itself, looming in front of me, showing off its new line of fall colors, goes unnoticed while my mind is engaged in squirrel talk. My sweater also goes unnoticed. It's been keeping me warm on this crisp morning. My glasses go unnoticed. They reveal sharp lines to the edges of leaves and allow me to see the alternating stripes on a chipmunk's back. As I notice, I learn about noticing and not noticing. I learn about attention.

Learning about attention has been an adventure for me, one full of surprises. I was surprised by the endless chatter of my mind. I was surprised by how often my attention is on myself, my feelings, thoughts, and ideas, rather than the world around me. I was surprised at how my attention shaped, actually became, my experience. But nothing was more surprising, truly shocking, than when I began to notice what I hadn't noticed. My early teachers were fallen trees.

Obstacles along the Way

On a sunny Sunday morning in April, I set out along a trail toward a magnificent promontory from which endless miles of Blue Ridge mountaintops could be viewed. The trail was rocky and ran along a creek, winding through a dense forest of pine, hemlock, and maple. Winter storms had strewn many trees and limbs across my path, creating unexpected detours.

After nearly three hours of effort I reached my destination. The view surpassed my expectations, and a cool breeze swept up the valley walls. As I enjoyed the view I recalled the difficulty involved in making my way past all of the fallen timber on the way up. One section of trail had resembled the hurdles event in the Olympics. At another junction stood a tree with its double trunk requiring a skillful slither above one trunk and below the other. How much easier my climb would have been had the fallen timber been cut away with a chain saw, leaving a pleasant, unobstructed path from beginning to end.

At that moment I vaguely recalled that some timber had, in fact, been cut away to clear the path. I remembered a few places in which a section of the trunk had been surgically removed, leaving the bottom and top of the tree resting unobtrusively on either side of the trail. How interesting that I could so clearly remember trees that blocked my way, but only with the greatest effort could I recall that there were obstacles that had been removed.

As I made my descent I noticed quite a few of these cut trees and decided to do some research. For a fifteen-minute period I counted both the trees that obstructed the path as well as those that had been cut to clear the way. The former were easy to count because they were in my way. If I didn't pay attention to them I'd trip over them. Noticing the latter, however, required additional concentration. I had to scan the borders of the trail for the cut ends of the logs. At the end of the sample period I counted forty-two obstacles. However, forty-seven trees had been cut to make the path easier! The reality was that during my ascent there were more trees cleared than left blocking the path. Yet it was the obstacles that dominated my memory of the experience.

For many of us, this hike resembles our lives. We notice the obstacles because we have to get around them to proceed. But what if we go through life only noticing obstacles, problems, and difficulties? Shouldn't we expect our experience to be one of anger, hurt, disappointment, and anxiety? What about the support, care, and kindness we receive each day? Through such awareness, we discover the invisible gifts of life. Trees that have been cleared magically reappear as kindness.

Self-Reflection

Those trees taught me about attention and self-reflection. They taught me how important it is to see life more accurately and precisely. I learned the significance of taking time to step back from myself and reflect on what I had noticed and had not noticed. If my response to the upward path was so skewed, what about my perspective for the past decades of my existence? What else had I missed? I was busy. I had things to do. Time for quiet, self-reflection seemed like a luxury. Yet I had a sense that my life was at stake. It was.

I was fortunate to discover a method of self-reflection that was developed in Japan. The concept of self-reflection is one that is endorsed by nearly everyone: religious leaders, therapists, educators, scientists, and others. Most people would say that self-reflection is a good idea, just as most people support the good ideas of love, peace, justice, and healthy living. But it is in method and practice that ideas become realities, and it is here that we must define and evaluate self-reflection. How do you actually reflect on yourself? What is the best method for examining your life?

The practice of self-reflection goes back many centuries and is rooted in the world's great spiritual traditions. Early adherents of such practice included the Christian desert hermits and Japanese samurai. More contemporary proponents include Albert Schweitzer, Benjamin Franklin, and Bishop Fulton J. Sheen. Franklin, in particular, had a rather comprehensive and systematic approach to self-reflection. He developed a list of thirteen virtues, and each day he would evaluate his conduct relative to a particular virtue. Daily self-reflection was a fundamental aspect of Franklin's life.

The type of self-reflection I am discussing involves certain basic characteristics. First, there is the requirement of time set aside exclusively for the purpose of self-reflection. Second, use of a space, preferably with some degree of isolation that limits external distraction. And third, the application of questions or a structure that helps us examine our lives with an emphasis on our conduct in relation to other people, creatures, and objects. A sincere examination of ourselves is not an easy task. It requires attention to what has not been attended to. It involves a willingness to squarely face our mistakes, failures, and weaknesses. It requires us to acknowledge our transgressions and actions that have caused difficulty to others. The fourth step of the Alcoholics Anonymous twelve-step program asks us to make a *searching and fearless moral inventory*. Albert Schweitzer's suggestion was to "make a secret account of what you have neglected in thoughtlessness or in meanness in consideration of some other person's existence." Such self-reflection leaves little room for blaming others or complaining about how we have been treated. Instead we are stripped naked of our excuses, rationalizations, and self-justification, leaving us to view our life as we have lived it. There is great power in reality as it is.

As human beings we possess the heartfelt desire to know ourselves and find meaning in our lives. And we have the capacity to do so. We may be the only creatures in the universe who can reflect on ourselves. We can observe our own thoughts and feelings and recall the actions and events of the past as if observing ourselves in a mirror. This capacity for self-reflection holds the key to our freedom while, at the same time, emerging from the roots of our own suffering.

Yet it is our suffering that awakens our desire for truth. It nudges, pricks, and pokes us with difficult questions and discontent. We can no longer be pacified by the accumulation of more "stuff." We become exhausted by a mind that constantly complains, criticizes, and judges others. Our dissatisfaction with ourselves and our lives spawns a sincere examination of that life.

So please join me on a journey of attention and self-reflection. Let's examine reality in a cup of tea. Let's study attention using our attention. Let's explore freshness in a candy wrapper and discover who taught us the ancient ritual of tying our shoes. Let's watch the film of our life to see how we have lived and how life lives through us. On this journey we'll destroy false myths, do battle with ego-centered dragons, get snared in traps of pride, and get stuck in the quicksand of selfishness. Yet even as we travel, our courage and effort are gifts, and the limited faith we have in ourselves is replaced by greater faith in life itself.

What Is Naikan?

Naikan is a Japanese word that means "looking inside," though a more poetic translation might be "seeing oneself with the mind's eye." It is a structured method of self-reflection that helps us to understand ourselves, our relationships, and the fundamental nature of human existence. Naikan was developed in Japan in the 1940s by Ishin Yoshimoto, a devout Buddhist of the Pure Land sect (Jodo Shinshu). His strong religious spirit led him to practice *mishirabe*, an arduous and difficult method of meditation and self-reflection. Wishing to make such introspection available to others, he developed Naikan as a method that could be more widely practiced.

> **"You are fooled by your mind into believing there is tomorrow, so you may waste today."**
> **ISHIN YOSHIMOTO**

Naikan's profound impact resulted in its use in other areas of Japanese society. Today, there are about forty Naikan centers in Japan, and Naikan is used in mental health counseling, addiction treatment, rehabilitation of prisoners, schools, and business. It has also taken root in Europe, with Naikan centers now established in Austria and Germany. In contrast to Japan, Naikan is relatively unknown in North America. David K. Reynolds, Ph.D., introduced Naikan to North America in the 1970s and later incorporated its framework into Constructive Living, an educational model that also includes elements of Morita Therapy. Reynolds was the first to write extensively about Naikan in English. Naikan programs and retreats have been offered regularly in the United States since 1989 by the TōDō Institute. But with the exception of a small number of adventurous Westerners who have wandered to Japan to study Naikan, or who have attended programs in North America and Europe, few Westerners have experienced and explored this Japanese practice of self-reflection.

Naikan broadens our view of reality. It's as if, standing on top of a mountain, we shift from a zoom lens to a wide-angle lens. Now we can appreciate the broader panorama; our former perspective is still included, but it is now accompanied by much that had been hidden. And what was hidden makes the view extraordinary.

The Three Questions

Naikan reflection is based on three questions:

What have I received from _____?

What have I given to _____?

What troubles and difficulties have I caused _____?

These questions provide a foundation for reflecting on all relationships, including those with parents, friends, teachers, siblings, work associates, children, and partners. You can reflect on yourself in relation to pets, or even objects such as cars and pianos. You can reflect on a specific period of time, one day or a holiday visit to your family. In each case, you acquire a more realistic view of your conduct and the give-and-take that has occurred in the relationship.

The questions themselves seem rather simple. They are. The depth of experience, insight, and realization that can come from the practice of self-reflection is not a result of intellectual analysis or complex theories. Our challenge is to just see reality as it is. These questions are simple inquiries for our investigation of life's mysteries and miracles.

The Journey Begins: The Care and Support You Received

Let's begin our inquiry with the first question: *What have I received from _____?*

In examining your relationship with another, begin by looking at what you have received from that person. My wife made me fresh-squeezed orange juice this morning. She washed my breakfast dishes. She gave me the watch I'm wearing. These are all simple, clear descriptions of reality. Her attitude or motivation does not change the fact that I benefited from her effort. Often we take such things for granted. We hurry through our day giving little attention to all the "little" things we are receiving. But are these things really little? They only seem so because, while we are being supported, our attention is elsewhere. But when there is no hot water for a shower or we lose our glasses, these little things grab our attention. Suddenly we are conscious of the true value of hot water and clear vision.

As you list what you have received from another person, you become grounded in the simple reality of how you have been supported and cared for. In many cases you may be surprised at the length or importance of the items on your list, and a deeper sense of gratitude and appreciation may be naturally stimulated. Your heart and mind begin to open to the grace that underlies all life. Without a conscious shift of attention to the myriad ways in which the world supports us, we risk our attention being trapped by problems and obstacles, leaving us to linger in suffering and self-pity.

So please take a few minutes now and begin making a list of what you have received during the past twenty-four hours. This type of daily reflection is called *daily Naikan (nichijo naikan* in Japanese). You are not limited to examining your relationship to one person, but can include anyone who supported you during the past day. Be specific and write down as many items as you can remember. What kind of food did you eat? Where did you go this past day? How did others support you? Did someone open a door? Did someone wash your dishes or was there hot water and soap available to you while washing dishes? What made it possible for you to brush your teeth or drive a car? Take ten minutes and make as thorough a list as possible. When you are done, please continue to the second question.

The Journey Continues: Your Contributions to Others

We now take a look at the second question: *What have I given to* _____?

Ishin Yoshimoto was a businessman. Each month he would send statements to his customers and receive similar statements from suppliers. These statements specified the products that were sent and the amount of money received. We receive a similar statement from the bank regarding our checking account. This tells us, to the penny, the balance in our account. Yoshimoto believed it was useful for human beings to conduct a similar examination of their "life balance." When you have examined, in detail, what you have given and received, you can determine this balance. You can compare your giving (credits) and taking (debits) in relation to a single person or between you and the rest of the world. You can examine a period of time ranging from a day to a decade.

This process is both a practical and spiritual reconciliation of our relationships with others. Does the world owe me or do I owe the world? Am I in debt to my mother or is she in debt to me? We often live our life as if the world owes us. "Why didn't I get that raise?" "Why is the pizza so late?" "How come I don't get more appreciation from my boss?" We resent it when people do not fulfill our expectations, living as if we deserve whatever we want. When people do support us, we often take their efforts for granted, living as if we were entitled to such efforts. As we reflect on our life we begin to see the reality of our life. What is more appropriate: to go through life with the mission of collecting what is owed us, or to go through life trying to repay our debt to others? Suppose I discover that I am the one who is in debt to the world. Such a realization kindles a natural desire to give and serve others and instills in me a greater sense of gratitude and realistic humility.

So please take another ten minutes and make a list of what you have given to others during the past twenty-four hours. Perhaps you gave someone a ride or prepared their dinner. Perhaps you sent a birthday card to a friend or picked up some litter on the street. Once again, be concrete and specific. Try to avoid generalizations like, "I was helpful" or "I was very supportive." What did you actually *do* for others?

The Final Question: The Troubles and Difficulties You Have Caused

Now you have a preliminary picture of your life for the past twenty-four hours. You have done some important research. Let's look at your lists. Have you been consistent? If you indicated that you gave a smile or thank-you to someone, have you also listed all the smiles and thank-yous you received from others? Have you been as accurate as possible? If you cooked someone a meal, have you also noted what you had to receive (for example, groceries, utensils, an oven, a recipe book) in order to cook for others? Take a few minutes and modify your lists, if necessary, so they more accurately reflect the reality of this past day.

The third and final question is the most difficult of all: *What troubles or difficulties have I caused _____?*

Mostly we are aware of how other people cause us inconvenience or difficulty. Perhaps somebody cuts us off in traffic, or maybe the person in front of us at the post office has a lot of packages and we are kept waiting. We notice such incidents with great proficiency. But when we are the source of the trouble or inconvenience, we often don't notice it at all. Or if we do, we think, "it was an accident" or "I didn't mean it." Perhaps we simply dismiss it as "not such a big deal." But this question is truly important. Yoshimoto suggested that when we reflect on ourselves, we spend at least 60 percent of the time considering how we have caused others trouble. His words are echoed by the lives of Franklin, Schweitzer, and St. Augustine. If we are not willing to see and accept those events in which we have been the source of others' suffering, then we cannot truly know ourselves or the grace by which we live.

Now please take another ten minutes and make a list of the troubles and difficulties you have caused others in the past twenty-four hours. Did you criticize someone? Did you leave dishes in the sink for someone else to wash? Did you keep someone waiting for a response to a letter or telephone call? Were you late for an appointment? Once again, please be specific.

Reflecting on Reflections

You have now completed your first research project; you have examined a small slice of your life (one day) in an attempt to see reality as clearly as possible. What can you learn from your research? Review your lists carefully. What are you aware of that you weren't aware of before? What have you taken for granted? What do you need to do and what do you need to do differently? This type of daily reflection, or daily Naikan, can been done before bedtime in twenty to thirty minutes. It is the simplest method of Naikan reflection. Throughout this book you will find many others.

Each exercise will give you an opportunity to examine a different aspect of your life—a different time period, relationship, or facet of your conduct.

We think we know our own life, but what we know is only an edited version, colored by our emotions and narrow vision. How close can we come to the original draft? Staring at truth, the soil is warmed, and we begin digging toward the sky.

AN EXAMPLE OF DAILY NAIKAN
A Day of Reflection

What Did I Receive?

1. My father bought a newspaper that I read.
2. Linda made me a fruit salad for breakfast.
3. The post office staff sorted my mail and put it in my box.
4. A toothbrush and toothpaste for brushing my teeth.
5. I wore a sweater that was a gift from my brother last Christmas.
6. The car, which took me to town and the airport safely.
7. The use of a pair of boots, a gift from Marilyn several years ago.
8. Linda washed the dinner dishes.
9. Eyeglasses, which allowed me to see more clearly.
10. Lines on the highway, which helped me (and others) to stay in the proper lanes and avoid accidents.
11. My father made me a cup of coffee.

12. My watch (an earlier gift from my wife) told me the time many times during the day.

13. Use of a meditation cushion made by Mrs. Tsuji.

14. Heat from oil and the furnace.

15. Fragrance and light from a candle (a gift from Mike Hall).

16. Use of the telephone lines and telephone service from the telephone company.

17. Barbara prepared book orders for mailing.

18. A deposit receipt from the bank.

19. A parking space in front of the municipal building.

20. A towel, soap, water, and a shower for showering.

21. Linda made the bed in the morning.

22. A pair of socks, which kept my feet warm during the day.

23. An axe to help me chop wood.

24. Use of a toilet for disposing of personal waste products.

25. A brush for brushing my hair.

26. Electricity provided me with light so I could work and read.

27. Chili, water, and a muffin from the staff at a local restaurant.

What Did I Give?

1. I walked and fed Rocky (our dog).

2. I drove my dad to the airport.

3. I watered two houseplants.

4. I massaged Linda's shoulders.

5. I gave $1.50 to the parking lot attendant.

6. I gave some fresh fruit to Linda to take to work.

7. I opened the door at the restaurant for a woman.

8. I took books to the post office for mailing to others.

9. I fed the birds.

10. I cleaned the bathroom.

11. I made Barbara a cup of tea.

What Troubles and Difficulties Did I Cause?

1. Two people called while I was out and had to talk to the answering machine.

2. I made a comment to my dad about the weather and airplanes that caused him some anxiety.

3. I talked about someone in a disrespectful way.

4. I put wear and tear on the car and tires by driving over one hundred miles (also on the roads).

5. I had several letters and two phone calls that remained unanswered.

6. I frightened a squirrel on the driveway when I was driving.

7. I continued to look at the newspaper while my father was talking to me.

8. While I tried to find the correct change at the airport parking lot, I kept several cars behind me waiting.

9. I wasted about one-eighth cup of coffee.

10. I displaced a community of ants by chopping a section of wood in which they had been living.

11. I forgot to turn the heat down when leaving the house and wasted fuel.

12. On two occasions I didn't turn my high beams down when an oncoming car was approaching.

Gratitude and the Practice of Attention and Reflection in Everyday Life

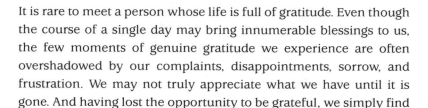

It is rare to meet a person whose life is full of gratitude. Even though the course of a single day may bring innumerable blessings to us, the few moments of genuine gratitude we experience are often overshadowed by our complaints, disappointments, sorrow, and frustration. We may not truly appreciate what we have until it is gone. And having lost the opportunity to be grateful, we simply find a new opportunity to be disappointed.

Gratitude requires attention and reflection. If we don't pay attention, the countless and constant ways we are supported go unnoticed. If we don't reflect, we fail to acquire the wisdom that comes with perspective.

> "If the only prayer you say your entire life is 'Thank you,' that would suffice."
>
> MEISTER ECKHART

The following essays may provide some insight into the experience of gratitude (and ingratitude). Included in this chapter are seven exercises that will help you go beyond the written words and work with these ideas in your own life. They ask that you pay attention and take time to reflect. When we begin to attend and reflect, ideas move from our head directly into our lives, and seeds of change are planted in the gardens of our experience.

Unwrapping Life's Gifts

I had dinner with Cathy in New York recently. Cathy is an attractive woman in her late fifties whom I have known for many years. During the course of our dinner Cathy proceeded to report on each of the key people in her life and describe how they were not meeting her needs and expectations. One of her good friends had failed to invite her to dinner, even though some other mutual friends had been invited. Her daughter and son-in-law did not allow her to spend enough time with her newborn grandchild. Her business partner was not attending to his work properly. Her husband had lost interest in making love to her. Her son had not sent her a birthday card. There were several others who fell short of her expectations. As she reported her stories I could see how much she was suffering. Just talking about all the people in her life this way resulted in an experience of suffering. I doubt that she even noticed what she was eating and who was serving it.

> "We pray for our daily bread; bread gives us the strength to do so."
>
> R. H. BLYTH

Cathy has an idea of what the

ideal friend would do, say, feel, think, and give. She has a similar image of the ideal son, daughter, husband, colleague, waiter, grocery clerk, and auto repair person. Each day she searches for her image of the ideal. Each day she experiences reality. Each day she focuses her attention on how reality fails to meet her image of the ideal. She has mastered the recipe for depression and disappointment. She has discovered a guaranteed formula for suffering. Over the years she has trained her mind to focus on the gap between her ideal of the world and her reality. Her mind has graduated with honors. It operates this way with less effort than it takes Cathy to brush her teeth. So Cathy suffers as each day brings her more disillusionment. With every story she reaches out for sympathy. But the sympathy others offer her pales in comparison with her ideal of the sympathy she wants.

How often have our minds played this same game? How often have we sunk into disappointment and resentment because others fell short of our ideals? We occupy a moment in time and a few cubic feet in space in a universe both timeless and without boundaries. And yet we believe that the universe should conform to our ideals. Can we be so arrogant as to think that such a cosmic speck is capable of knowing what is truly ideal?

As long as we hold fast to our ideal of what we deserve from the world we blind ourselves to the gifts we *are* receiving. We look back on our childhood and notice what could have been done for us and given to us that, we think, would have made us happier. The gap between our reality and our ideal of what it should have been like attracts our attention like a magnet. But to focus on this gap is to miss most of reality. We miss the countless moments when we were perfectly cared for and attended to. We trade the reality of how we were loved for the illusion that we should have been loved more and better. It's an unworthy exchange that leads us to spiritual and emotional bankruptcy.

When I narrow my vision to search for an ideal that my mind has created, life seldom complies. But when I broaden my vision to simply notice what life is offering, I find that I am surrounded by an abundance of care and support. Yet, we can repeatedly observe the mechanics of a mind that is rarely satisfied with what it has at the moment because it is always yearning for some manufactured ideal. We can witness eyes that scan reality for what they want, failing to see what they are being offered. Such awareness is the first step in retraining ourselves to truly open to the gifts the universe is offering to us.

Have you ever seen a young child who has a single, rigid idea of what he wants for Christmas? On Christmas morning he rapidly unwraps all his gifts, looking for the single gift his mind has targeted. In the absence of this item he cries, sulks, and pouts as he walks away from the Christmas tree in disappointment. In his wake he leaves all of his presents, abandoned and unappreciated. How often does this pouting, spoiled child surface in our own daily encounters with life? How many gifts have we left lying under the Christmas trees of our past? How many presents remain unwrapped because we have failed to even notice their presence?

Take a moment, Cathy, to reclaim your gifts and abandon your ideal images. You have it backward. Open your eyes and see how many gifts there are to unwrap. Notice the presence of your presents. It's not your life that is disappointing: it's your mind.

Exercise #1

Spend an hour reflecting on the past year of your life. What are the most important things you've received this past year? Who made these gifts possible?

- Did you have some form of transportation? Who made this possible?
- Did you have a roof over your apartment or house? Who made this possible?
- Did you receive any medical or dental treatment? Who made this possible?
- Did you receive any new or used clothing? Who made this possible?
- Did you receive information or entertainment from television, newspapers, movies, etc.?

See how many items you can list, and for each item list some of the people involved in making it possible. As you list these items, consider what your life would have been like without them. At the end of the hour, carefully review your list and reflect on the nature of your life this past year.

You Saved My Life

Suppose you are on a boat and there is an accident. You find yourself struggling to stay above the icy, rough sea as wave after wave pushes you under. Suddenly a lifeboat appears next to you and an older woman helps you into the boat. What would your attitude be toward this woman? How would you feel about her? What would you say to her? What would you do for her when you were safely back on shore? Could you ever do enough to repay her for saving your life?

Your life is being saved at this very moment. Each moment. Each breath. You may not notice it, yet ten, twenty, or thirty times a minute your life is saved by the life-giving air that you are breathing. Take a deep breath. Notice the air going deep into your lungs. Your body takes what it needs to survive. Once again, your life is saved. What is your attitude toward air? What have you done for air lately? Could you ever do enough to repay it for giving you life? What trouble have you caused the air that continually saves your life?

Sometimes I have an opportunity to swim in a pond on a hot summer day. I swim the length of the pond underwater, not coming up for air until I reach the other side. By the time I have finished my breathless lap, I am desperate for the air I have denied myself. As my head anxiously breaks the water's surface, I gasp for a deep drink of life-saving air. How wonderful it feels to take in air again, to feel it rushing into my lungs and have it carried to my limbs. Again I breathe. And again. My body relaxes as blood rushes through my arteries with express deliveries of oxygen wherever it is needed.

But what if I came up for a passionate gasp of air and there was no air available? The deepest, most desperate breath would be in vain. How long before I would die? But of course that has never happened. Whether I was kind or selfish that day, whether I spoke gently or abruptly, whether I treated others lovingly or cruelly, the air was always there to greet me and save my life. I

> **"Every day is a good day."**
> UMMON

depend on it and it has proven itself dependable. Its dependability nourishes faith and trust. *Thank you,* air.

But it isn't only air that saved my life today. Water also deserves this recognition. Most of my body consists of water, which is constantly replenished by food and drink. And my heart keeps beating without rest. Even when I take a coffee break, my heart does not. And my lungs and every essential organ in my body work together in ways I don't even understand so I can breathe and speak and urinate. And then there's heat. And sunlight.

I slept fairly well last night, even though I didn't try to sleep well. When I try to sleep well I usually don't sleep well at all. It seems more accurate, more realistic, to consider a good night's sleep a gift. Thank you, water. Thank you, lungs. Thank you, sleep. Thank you, bed.

I am truly humbled when I realize that living beings died today so that I might continue to live. Today a potato, a tomato, some wheat, lettuce, rice, a banana, and blueberries lost their lives for my sake. Some of this food died on farms hundreds of miles away. But I must admit that I killed the tomato myself. I kidnapped it from its mother tomato bush. It had little time to say its final good-byes as it left the plant that nurtured and carried its weight ever since it was born. We had a quiet stroll from garden to kitchen. Then I sliced it up and ate it in a bowl full of lettuce. It is now me. Together, we'll plant tomato seeds next spring. Thank you, tomato. I'm sorry, tomato. I owe you my life, our life.

Autumn arrives and blushing tomatoes have been replaced by apples. Still, I miss the tomatoes. There is something about deprivation that wakes us up to appreciation. Even words are appreciated more when they are not available. During a day of silence at our residential training program, we continue to go about our daily business. We cook, clean, and go to the supermarket, but without speaking. Since we aren't speaking, we write notes or try to communicate nonverbally. This requires a great deal of time and effort. Even ordering a loaf of rye bread at the local bakery becomes complicated and confusing. I realize how much easier my life is because I have been given the gift of speech. If you've been to a non-English-speaking country you know how difficult it can be to conduct your daily affairs without words. Thank you, speech. Thank you, words. Thanks to my parents and all my teachers who taught me how to speak English. Speech is a remarkable gift.

And yet, silence is also a gift. The absence of talk creates an atmosphere in which I notice sounds that often go unnoticed. I hear the chickadees singing in the yard. I hear the wind wrestling with the TV antenna on the roof. I hear the footsteps of people walking and water rushing from a faucet. It is not just that the quiet brings these sounds to life; it is that my mind no longer feels pressured to speak in response to the activity around me. I realize how much I miss as I am formulating a response in my mind. Not speaking helps us notice the gift of words. Silence helps us notice the songs of birds. Swimming helps us notice the gift of breath. Fasting helps us appreciate the nourishment and value of food. Separation from the people we love helps us notice the blessings of their companionship.

Deprivation can stimulate appreciation. Such experiences remind us how difficult life would be in the absence of reality's gifts. Yet how much better it is to appreciate what we have at the very moment it is here. Why wait till these gifts are gone? Why reminisce over pleasant memories rather than appreciating what we have now, before it becomes a memory? Of course, we know this intellectually. But our intellect is powerless to guide us to real gratitude and appreciation. The *practice* of attention and reflection allows us to begin this journey.

Exercise #2

For the next week, spend thirty minutes each night before bedtime doing daily Naikan reflection as described on page 31. Make a list in response to each of the three questions:

What did I receive from others today? (10 minutes)
What did I give to others today? (10 minutes)
What troubles and difficulties did I cause others today? (10 minutes)

Be specific and don't leave out the little things (hint: there are no little things).

At the end of the week review your daily lists and write a thank-you note to one person for something specific that that person did for you or gave to you.

Ordering a Pizza

Many of us, at one time or another, have ordered a pizza and had it delivered to our home. Let's do some detective work and try to trace its origins. Perhaps, while we're at it, we can learn something about the art of awareness.

We begin by picking up a plastic object called a telephone and dialing seven one-digit numbers. Even that is easier than it used to be because many people now have Touch-Tone phones rather than dial phones. And if we have automatic dialing, it may take only one little push of the finger before we're in touch with the restaurant.

In less than an hour there is a delivery person knocking at the door with a pizza. How did that happen? Well, this person took the pizza from the restaurant to the car and drove all the way to our home to bring us our pizza. He went out of his way to find our house or apartment, perhaps in the dark. Fortunately, someone made a map of our neighborhood. He had to risk his life driving a car in traffic. People are killed every day driving cars. Delivery people are robbed delivering pizzas. He risked his life and welfare so we could have a pizza.

Of course, someone made and baked the pizza. And others assembled, sold, and maintained the delivery car. Someone constructed the ovens so the pizza could be baked. Electricity was needed to operate the ovens. People built the pizza restaurant. Someone paid for the advertising so we could look up the phone number in the telephone directory. Or perhaps we called directory assistance and received help from some stranger who was willing to give us the correct phone number. An entire telecommunications system allowed us to call and say, "What's the phone number of the Pizza Place?"

What about the ingredients themselves? Where did the crust come from? How is cheese produced? What

> "It is the familiar that usually eludes us in life. What is before our nose is what we see last."
>
> WILLIAM BARRETT

about tomato sauce? What's involved in getting sauce to the restaurant from a tiny tomato seed somewhere on a farm? Ingredients came from all over the country, maybe even the world. Plants were nourished by sun and rain and harvested by farmers and delivered by truck drivers. Factories were built to package the ingredients. Cans were made to preserve their contents.

Roads, trucks, cars, factories, phone lines, plants, dirt, sun and rain, cows—all and more were made use of—so we can open the door and find a pizza ready to eat. And it's hot. Someone even put it in a box for us. Part of a tree sacrificed its life so we could get our pizza in a box. The history of an entire universe is revealed by a cardboard box. Close your eyes and read it.

Then we sit down and eat, and it's pretty tasty. And we did so little for that pizza. All we had to do was press the buttons on our phone, say, "we'd like a pizza," and pay money that someone was kind enough to give to us in the first place.

What an incredible and complex process it is to receive a pizza. And yet how often is such a gift ignored! How often is our response, "How come it took so long? They said it would only take thirty minutes and it took forty-five minutes." Or perhaps, "It's not hot enough. It should be hotter than this." Or maybe we begin to eat and we notice it has green peppers and we say, "I didn't order green peppers. Why did they put these stupid green peppers on my pizza? Now I'll have to pick them all off." Perhaps we call the restaurant to complain. How often have we called and said, "I just wanted to let you know how much I liked the pizza you made for me."

Isn't this just a microcosm of much of our life? Despite all the effort that went into giving us that pizza, our attention shifts to the fact that it isn't "perfect." Our mind scouts around and embraces something that doesn't quite meet our expectations. But frequently it is perfect: everything came out the way we like it. So now what do we do? Mostly, we don't do anything. We eat. We don't even notice this perfect pizza right in front of us. We're too busy watching the movie or reading or talking with other people.

Maybe we deserve a hot, fast, fresh, tasty pizza. Maybe we're entitled to friendly, helpful service from the person who takes our order. Maybe it's our right to have everything come out perfect according to our desires. If we conclude that we have always perfectly fulfilled the desires, needs, and expectations of those around us, then we have reason to expect the same from the world. But as I reflect on the ways in which I have caused trouble, the times I've been late, the times I've made mistakes, the rarity with which I've done a "perfect" job for others—as I reflect on these things, I cannot help but be deeply touched by all the effort that went into bringing me a pizza. So to those people and objects who have been responsible for all the pizzas I have received since I was a child, Thank you! I may not know who you are, but I know what you did.

Exercise #3

Next time you have a meal from a restaurant, call them later and thank them, telling them what you liked about the meal or how it was helpful to you (for example, since they cooked for you, you were able to get other things done).

In the Midst of Pain

Once, not long ago, it was a hearty tree
providing shade, food, and oxygen—
a world of its own.

For a hundred years,
perhaps more,
it flourished with breath and life.

Then it was cut, sawed, ground, and pressed
until it found itself resting softly
between two friends.

Peacefully and patiently
it waited for the moment
it would burst forth into the world
and exercise the meaning of its life.

And now that moment has come.
It gracefully caresses my cheek,
wiping the tears from my eyes
and taking on my pain as its own

All those years
as seed, tree, wood
and tissue
in preparation for the fleeting moment
it would console my sadness.

As it gives its life to comfort me
I almost failed to see the kindness in its deed.

Wrapped up in self-centered pain, tear-blinded,
I nearly missed its selfless service.
Who will give witness to such compassion if not me?

Shriveled and soaked, it died while serving a fool
who discarded thousands of its brothers and sisters
without a thanks—not one tear shed in gratitude.

Teach me to see through the teardrop, that in the midst of pain
I may understand the true source
of the softness against my face.

Teach me to cry with my eyes wide open.

Naikan at Work

Jill arrived for her weekly session expressing anger and frustration about an incident that occurred at work the day before.

Her company's parking lot is attended by a young man and locked each evening at 6:00 p.m. Everyone is required to move their car out of the lot by 6:00 p.m. if they are working late. The lot is then locked up and the attendant goes home. On one occasion Jill was delayed and could not get to the lot until 6:20 p.m. The lot was locked, so she could not get her car out, but the attendant was still there. She apologized for being late and asked him to open the gate so she could get her car out. He refused. He said the lot was closed. She reiterated her apology and explained what had happened. He still refused to open the gate. Finally she summoned one of her superiors to come down to the lot and "order" the attendant to open the gate. She was absolutely furious about the incident.

At the end of her session I gave her an assignment for the following week. Her assignment was to buy the attendant a gift. A gift? Needless to say she was not happy with the assignment. Why would I ask her to buy a gift for someone who had caused her so much grief?

That the attendant refused to let her remove her car from the parking lot is reality. I do not deny it. But there is another reality, the reality of his daily supervision of the parking lot and her car for as long as she has been working there. Her car has never been stolen, vandalized, or damaged in any way. Her attention was well focused on the first reality, the trouble he caused her, but she missed the second, his longtime service.

Naikan, simply stated, helps us to see other people and the world around us more realistically. We notice that the secretary who seems to take such long lunches also worked until 10:00 p.m. last Friday night to finish that important report. The supervisor who criticizes our work also defended us in front of the division manager. As we see the reality of our life, our view of the support we're getting from others is included.

In Japan, if you give awards to individual employees, it may embarrass them. They might say they don't deserve it; that the accomplishment belongs to many people who contributed to the effort. They're not just being modest, they're being truthful. In the United States we're more likely to believe that it was really "my success," "my achievement alone."

A successful businessman was

> **"Usually thinking is rather self-centered. In our everyday life our thinking is ninety-nine percent self-centered: Why do I have suffering? Why do I have trouble?"**
> SHUNRYU SUZUKI ROSHI

studying Naikan. Despite his success, he felt something was missing from his life. He was often depressed and frequently had difficulty with personal and family relationships. Still, he was very proud of all that he had accomplished. He was particularly proud of how he had made it on his own, without the help of anybody. I asked him to list his five greatest accomplishments for his next session. When he met with me the next week, I found he had listed *eight*. For the next two months I asked him to consider one accomplishment each week in light of the following questions:

> *What support or help did I receive from others (people, objects, etc.) in order to accomplish this?*
>
> *What did my accomplishment do for others?*
>
> *In the process of working toward this accomplishment, what troubles and difficulties did I cause others*

It was a difficult and emotional effort for him. Each week he did his Naikan reflection and was faced with the reality that his accomplishments were not really his. He consistently identified a wealth of support and assistance he had been given. He realized how the efforts of others had made these accomplishments possible. His wife, colleagues, secretary, and employees all provided him with support that was essential to his work. He also realized, for the first time, how much trouble these accomplishments had caused *others*. He began to see the impact his long hours of work had had on his family. He tried to understand what it must have been like to be an employee who was always criticized and never commended. And while he had derived many benefits from his achievements, he had difficulty finding many ways in which he had supported others during the course of his work.

A part of him was dejected, saddened to see that self-made was more accurately "other-made." He also realized how self-centered he had been, taking so much and giving so little. And yet there was also a part of him that was overjoyed by the world's support of his work and his life all these years. Knowing he hadn't done it alone was a refreshing insight. Along with his feelings of guilt came feelings of gratitude, a sense of appreciation for those around him.

We live under the illusion of independence. The boundaries of our job description, our title, our office walls, and our projects reinforce the idea that we can and do work independently from others. Nothing could be further from the truth. Our work is *completely* dependent on others. Is there any tangible work product that we can produce without relying on the products and efforts of others? The music we write is only an arrangement of notes created by others. Teamwork is not an option for our work situation, it's the reality. Such awareness may lead to a desire to thank and repay people for all of their support. Success invites an expression of gratitude to others rather than self-congratulations. The conditions of our work environment can shift from conflict to cooperation as we notice the way *the* work, not *our* work, gets done.

Exercise #4

Choose an accomplishment you are proud of. It could be graduating from college, learning a foreign language, or winning some type of award. Now, using this accomplishment as a focal point, spend one hour reflecting on the three questions listed above.

Looking beyond Our Difficulties

Periodically we find ourselves in very challenging circumstances. We lose our jobs, get sick, experience the death of a loved one, or end a long-term relationship. We become immersed in our own pain, and our minds notice all the disappointing elements of our lives.

Our attention seems to become trapped within the limited boundaries of our suffering. But there is more to life than we are seeing. As we expand our view of life we may find that even within the context of our suffering, compassion, care, and support are our close companions. When we reflect upon such circumstances, we see it is often due to the support of others that we were able to resolve or recover from our problem. But how often do we make room for gratitude in the midst of our suffering? Even in the aftermath of recovery from a serious illness or resolution of an important problem, how much energy goes to thanking and repaying those people who, and things that, supported us during our time of need?

When we expand the boundaries of our attention we see a larger, more truthful picture of life. A life that is continuing to support us throughout our difficult moments. A life that is actually helping us to deal with our difficulties.

> Shrouded in a cloud
> of depression
> Thoughts of what's
> going wrong,
> One after another.
> HO SEN

Taking Things for Granted

One of the high points upon my return from Southeast Asia was flushing my toilet. I generally don't pay much attention to flushing the toilet. Neither do most Westerners, I suspect. But this was the first time in weeks I had used a toilet that flushed. In much of Southeast Asia there is an alternative method in which you dip a bowl in an urn of clean water and pour it into the toilet. You do this several times until the clean water has replaced the old water. It works quite well and conserves water, though it takes more effort than a flush toilet. I was standing in my bathroom, watching the toilet flush, and I realized how easy it was just to flip a lever, walk away, and know that when I returned the water in the toilet would be clear and fresh. You might say that a flush toilet is something I have taken for granted. But, more accurately, it is something I have *not* taken for granted.

To grant is to give. A foundation may grant money to a charitable organization. You may grant me permission to use your car. To take something for granted is to take something as given. But I have never considered a flush toilet as given. I have just used flush toilets inattentively and ungratefully all my life. The most attention I have given them was in planes and trains, where you have to search for the lever or button that flushes the toilet. If the location of this triggering device wasn't immediately obvious, I might silently comment on a more likely spot for its placement. But I never took the toilet for granted, I would simply *take* the service it provided without a moment of thought and move on to my next activity.

As it turns out, a man by the name of Thomas Crapper (honestly) developed the Valveless Water Preventer for toilets in the late nineteenth century.

> "No matter what food you are blessed with, if you weren't blessed with an appetite too, you'd be in a bad way, wouldn't you?"
> KOSHO UCHIYAMA ROSHI

His invention resulted in much greater conservation of London's limited water supply. As a result of his invention he was actually *knighted*. So I am able to flush my toilet thanks, in part, to an English plumber-knight who was creative and persistent enough to invent a new mechanism for clearing the toilet of dirty water.

And what about the many other devices I *take* without considering them granted. I wonder about the years of human lives that went into developing dimmer switches for my lights, locks for my doors, contact lenses for my eyes. Combing my hair, my attention is lost in vanity and seldom leaves room for the recognition of efforts that have given me a mirror and comb. I wish I could take more things as *granted,* using them with an awareness that they are gifts born of the lives and sacrifices of others. To remember this is to bring my attention to certain truths that too often fall outside the boundaries of my awareness. Whether I notice or not, I continue to benefit from the efforts and accomplishments of those whose bodies have long since disappeared. Their services remain and should be received and appreciated as granted.

Exercise #5

Throughout the day notice the objects that support you in your daily life: a toilet, a coffeemaker, a can opener, etc. Before going to bed make a list of these objects. Reflect on the efforts it took to invent, design, manufacture, package, and ship these objects so they might make your life a bit easier or more enjoyable.

Itadakimasu

The Japanese often put their hands together in prayerlike fashion before a meal and recite a short Japanese phrase, *Itadakimasu*. I had difficulty remembering this phrase until someone suggested a memory technique—"eat a duck, I must." Ironically, though I am a vegetarian, I would find myself thinking of this phrase as I began each meal. Still, this helped me remember to accurately recite *itadakimasu* before eating. Sometime later *itadakimasu* was translated into English for me. In general, it means "I humbly receive (this food)." But the experience of *itadakimasu* is made special when the palms are placed together (called *gassho* in Japanese) and the head is bowed. There is something about the attitude of the head bowed, the eyes lowered, and the hands in *gassho* that gives depth to the recitation of *itadakimasu*. There seems to be greater mindfulness of the true meaning of the words. I later discovered that another translation of *itadakimasu* is, "I receive by putting on my head." This emphasizes the respect we offer to what we are receiving by raising it up, even as we lower ourselves. We raise the food out of respect for its sacrifice to us. Living things have died and are now being offered for our benefit. We lower ourselves by acknowledging that we are benefiting from the sacrifice of these living beings. We are taking and others are giving.

Those who have been raised in a Judeo-Christian culture may compare *itadakimasu* to the grace that is often said before meals. So uttering *itadakimasu* may seem no more unusual

> **"If you are a poet, you will see clearly that there is a cloud floating in this sheet of paper."**
> THICH NHAT HANH

than saying grace. But the other day a student of mine called. She had recently been introduced to Naikan and responded enthusiastically to much of what she read. But she was a bit uncomfortable acknowledging the support of objects. And she "drew the line when it came to saying thank you to objects." She gave the example of thanking one's socks when one is cleaning out a sock drawer, an exercise sometimes given to students studying Constructive Living. To her, thanking one's socks seemed silly and inappropriate. Many Americans would smile and agree.

One reason we find it strange to thank objects is that they can't hear or understand us. At least we assume that is true. I remember the story of a woman who was very resentful toward several nurses after coming out of a coma. She remembered her nurses talking insultingly about her during their daily visits to her room. Most of us believe that people who are sleeping, in a coma, or dead can't hear us. Yet we often talk to them anyway. How many mothers have said good night to a sleeping child? How many loved ones at a funeral have said good-bye or I love you to the one departed? It sounds a bit strange, but in the moment when we are saying these things, it often seems natural and appropriate. Still, it may seem awkward to say thank you to a pair of socks.

Perhaps our reluctance to thank things has to do with the distinctions we make. We distinguish the socks (inanimate) from the cotton plants, farmers, and factory workers (animate) who created them. We may be willing to thank the latter, but to thank the former seems silly. Many Westerners who say grace are thanking God, not the food itself, for the meal. God deserves our thanks, but to thank the food would be strange. We'll thank the mechanic for repairing our car, but to thank the car directly for taking us to work seems absurd. As long as these distinctions hold up, we can remain safely within these boundaries of gratitude.

But do they hold up? What are socks anyway? Are they anything less than the life efforts of the plants and people who made them? A cotton plant's life is the source of these socks. Farmers, factory workers, delivery people, and others gave moments of their lives to make these socks. These socks are full of life! If I subtract all the life from the making of these socks, there would be nothing left. It is true that they do not have a heartbeat. But they serve me just the same. Acting most unselfishly, they go wherever I take them, shielding my feet and softening my steps upon the earth. I have several pairs of thick cotton socks that provide a cozy blanket against our bare wood floors during the frigid Vermont winters. When I am mindful of the service socks offer me and the efforts that went into making them, I am thankful. Yet there is still this sticky problem of whether to *say* thanks to a pair of socks.

The best reason I can offer for saying thank you to socks is that they deserve it. Doesn't anything that serves, supports, and cares for us deserve a word of thanks? But here's another reason. Saying thank you to people and things will change your experience of life. Each moment we say thanks is a shift in our attention. A shift away from our self-centeredness toward others. A shift away from our problems and difficulties toward the support we are receiving from the world. Our attention is our life. Shifting our attention opens us to reality and reveals what has been there all along: socks.

Exercise #6

Mindful thank-yous. For the next three days, say thank you to who-
ever gives you something. When you say thank you, make sure you
mention the item or service for which you are expressing thanks.
For example, "Thank you, Jim, for helping me move the sofa." Or,
"Thank you for bringing me more coffee." This phrasing helps us
avoid "mindless" thank-yous in which we say the words but pay little attention to the person or service.

The Expression of Gratitude

To live a life of gratitude is to open our eyes to the countless ways in
which we are supported by the world around us. Such a life provides less space for our suffering because our attention is more balanced. We are more often occupied with noticing what we are
given, thanking those who have helped us, and repaying the world
in some concrete way for what we are receiving and have received
in the past. Our minds are absorbed by noticing and reflecting; our
bodies are kept busy expressing and repaying. If you have been
doing the exercises at the end of each essay, you are already developing a healthy foundation for awareness and action. Perhaps you
are more aware of repaired potholes in a road or someone opening
the door for you at the store. But perhaps there are also times when
you notice such things and still don't feel grateful. What should you
do when your expanded awareness still leaves you feeling upset,
depressed, or resentful?

It is important to distinguish between the internal experience
of gratitude (thoughts and feelings) and the expression of gratitude

in the form of words, thank-you notes, services, or gifts. We may receive something and not feel grateful. It is not necessary to struggle to create such a feeling. We simply feel what we feel. Such feelings are beyond our power, and it is a misuse of effort to try to fight our feelings of ingratitude or create feelings of gratitude. Rather, we should respond with an *expression* of gratitude, such as a verbal thanks, a letter, or a gift. Those who have supported us deserve our attention and our thanks. Such actions are possible even where there is an absence of felt gratitude. Often it is the active acknowledgment of what we have received that stimulates true feelings of gratitude. Our efforts to reciprocate by offering a gift or service of our own may actually awaken us to the experience of gratitude. But if we "go after" such a feeling, we become preoccupied with our own comfort and pleasure. Naikan simply asks us to be aware of reality, and our gratitude is *expressed* because it is *deserved* by others.

Are we willing to examine our own lives and see how often we have failed to express gratitude for what we have received? This is dangerous territory, for it is uncomfortable to acknowledge our own ingratitude. But through such an investigation we can become aware of the mechanics of ingratitude and perhaps bring more appreciation into our own life as well as the lives of others.

From my own personal experience here are eleven reasons for failing to express gratitude:

> "You must learn to understand the secret of gratitude. It is more than just so-called virtue. It is revealed to you as a mysterious law of existence. In obedience to it we have to fulfill our destiny."
> ALBERT SCHWEITZER

1. **Misdirected attention.** I fail to express gratitude because I do not notice what is being given to me. Where is/was my attention? When my attention is on myself—my worries, my pain, my dreams, my troubles—then it is not possible to attend to all the gifts life is bringing me each moment. At times when I am sick or my car is not working, I find it is common for me to focus on my problem so intently that I fail to notice and acknowledge the help I am receiving from others.

2. **Lack of reflection.** Sometimes I am not truly aware of what I have received until I have taken a moment to reflect on my life in a concrete way. Such reflection helps me to see all the ways I have benefited in a particular situation. It helps me to understand the degree of trouble to which others have gone. It helps me to see how my life is better as the result of a small gift or service. Such reflection, whether a momentary pause or a formal period of Naikan, often inspires me to express my gratitude. Without reflection, I am not truly aware of the magnitude of the support I am receiving.

3. **My assumption that others must "know" how grateful I am.** Sometimes I feel gratitude but I fail to express it because I assume that the other person must know that I am grateful. This is most common when the other person is someone with whom I am intimately acquainted. In such cases I seem most likely to forgo a thank-you because I suspect the other person knows me so well that she surely is aware of my gratitude. Yet this isn't always the case. Even if it was, the expression of gratitude is still preferable. I cannot recall one instance where I have regretted sending a thank-you note or saying the words "thank you."

4. **Procrastination.** Too often I have said to myself, "I must send that person a thank-you note," and waited until so much time had passed that I abandoned my good intentions.

At the moment I am in receipt of a kindness, the feeling of gratitude is often strongest. Yet I so quickly become preoccupied with other things that the importance of the kind act fades and I lose sight of its value and the effort on the part of the person who supported me. Though it is best to say thank you promptly, I am usually delighted to receive a note indicating that someone I helped still recalls the incident months or even years later. It's never too late for gratitude.

5. **Forgetting**. Unless I make a note of it, I am likely to forget to express my gratitude. Verbal thank-yous can be offered immediately, but gifts and letters must often wait at least a few hours. Notes and lists are good secretaries. The recent addition of a thank-you log on my refrigerator door helps compensate for my poor memory.

6. **Laziness**. Sometimes it is clearly a question of giving in to my own physical or mental laziness. When I consider the little effort required to send a thank-you note as compared with the greater effort made on my behalf in the first place, it saddens me to think that I have benefited from the greater effort while failing to make the lesser.

7. **My entitlement:** Sometimes my mind tells me that I have a right to what I received, and therefore gratitude is unnecessary. This is particularly true in situations where I have provided payment to the other party and feel that I am entitled to what I received. Yet the truth is that I am twice indebted. First to those who provided me with money and second to those who provide me with goods or services. In neither case am I entitled, yet in both cases I am the recipient of another's support.

8. **They were just doing their duty.** My mind will also attempt to relieve me of a need to express gratitude by suggesting that this person was just doing his job, something he needed

to do anyway. So why should I express gratitude for something he has given since it is required of him? Yet regardless of his motivation, I am still benefiting from his effort, and it is the benefit I receive that is the only prerequisite for an expression of gratitude.

9. **It wasn't much trouble for them.** My mind may tell me that gratitude is unnecessary because the effort of the other person was not much trouble for her. But even a simple gift or service may have required more trouble than I can know. Perhaps she sent me a copy of an article and had to search at great length for a copy machine. Or perhaps she went out of her way to take it to the post office when she was in a hurry. That I received something is justification enough for my gratitude to be expressed.

10. **The person later causes me some trouble or difficulty.** If I receive something from another human being and that person later does something that causes me trouble, does that erase the original act of kindness and service? Of course not. Perhaps a business is late in delivering an order, though previous orders were delivered on time. No matter what they do, I have still benefited from their prior service. In these cases I am likely to feel very little gratitude. I am more likely to feel anger or resentment. But it is just these moments that allow me to reflect on the reality of their earlier efforts and services. Schweitzer states that "The person to whom you owe a debt of gratitude may never be allowed to become just a person like any other to you; he remains someone special for you, like something that is holy to you."

11. **The giftgiver is gone or unknown.** Often it is not possible to express gratitude to someone who has made our life better because we do not know the name or whereabouts of the person. I have some rosebushes in the backyard. I expect they were planted by one of the previous owners of my

home, but I have no idea who it was or whether he or she is even alive today. Yet each year I cut roses from these bushes and put them in a vase in my office. How can I express my gratitude for such a lovely, ongoing gift?

Well, I can take good care of the rosebushes. I think such care is one method of showing gratitude to the person who put many hours into growing and nurturing them, before they became my companions. I can also plant some additional rosebushes for those who will live in this house when I am gone. Of course this will not benefit the original planter, but if I look closely I can see that the source of this gift is much broader. It includes the sun, rain, soil, truck driver, fertilizer company, and many others. As I see the many ways in which the universe has offered me a rose, my gratitude is appropriately broadened beyond one person. This is true for the rose, as well. For even though I may be watering and pruning it, it blooms and offers its beauty and fragrance to all who will take a moment to pay attention.

Exercise #7

This exercise involves reflection exclusively on our relationship with one other person. In Japan, this is the most traditional approach to Naikan, and we usually begin by reflecting on our relationship with our mother. If you prefer, you may reflect on your relationship with your father, spouse, teacher, best friend, or any other significant person. You will examine the entire history of the relationship, but you divide the time into shorter periods. If you are reflecting on a parent, you begin by examining the period from your birth until you were nine years old. Then you proceed in three-year segments. If you are examining your relationship with

The Train

The train just keeps moving.
No matter what route you take, there are no stops.
There's just the ride.

Many passengers—one destination.
The man next to me says,
    "They should fix the track, the ride is too bumpy."
He's sitting next to me but he's on a different train.
He says to the conductor,
    "Are we there yet?"
"No, we're here now."

Wherever we go, the scenery travels in the other direction.
I miss so much when I blink.
Falling to sleep, the trip seems quicker.
I'd rather stay awake.
I want to see every little town, every road, every leaf on every
tree.

The conductor keeps me awake.
How kind of him. Even my ticket was a gift.

Now the swsssshhhh of a dark tunnel.

your husband or wife, the segments might be one or two years, depending on how long you have been married. The three Naikan questions (what have I received, what have I given, and what troubles have I caused) provide a structure for you to examine the relationship. Each day, reflect for one hour on a different period until you have covered the entire relationship from beginning until the present day. Then review your lists and reflect on the nature of your relationship. Is there some way to express your appreciation for what was given to you?

SAMPLE NAIKAN REPORT

A Man Reflects on Moving into a New House

Moving from one house or apartment can be an overwhelming task that leaves you feeling exhausted and focused on all the problems you encountered. In such a situation it's easy to overlook all the support and help that you received to relocate your life from one place to another. In the following example, a man reflects on his experience during several days of packing and moving. Consider how this type of self-reflection might change your attitude and perception of a challenging experience.

What Did I Receive?

1. My friend Ron came and helped load the truck and then unloaded it. (About nine hours.)
2. My friend Dave also helped load and unload the truck. (About nine hours.)
3. A guy named Ed, whom my wife knew from work, helped load and unload the truck and then came back the next day to help finish the job. (About twelve hours.)
4. Ed built a ramp up to the deck so it would be easier to unload things.

5. The service station reserved the biggest U-Haul available for me and provided a dolly and pads and gasoline and instruction on driving the truck.

6. When the truck wouldn't start the second day, the U-Haul company arranged for a service person to come and jump the battery.

7. Ron helped figure out the best way to get the piano out of the house and into the truck.

8. All the drivers stayed on their side of the road while I was driving to the new house.

9. My friends Jiun and Banzan stopped by for a day at the end of their vacation and helped us pack boxes, even though they were moving overseas and needed to return to New York to do their own packing.

10. Our landlady was very flexible and allowed us to keep some things in the garage after the date by which we were to vacate the house.

11. There was good weather on the day we moved.

12. I received the use of gloves when I was loading the truck.

13. I was able to drive the truck because my dad taught me how to drive a stick shift and later arranged for me to get a job working for his company driving a delivery truck.

14. My eyeglasses allowed me to see more clearly.

15. My watch allowed me to keep track of the time.

16. My wife did a lot of packing and made lunch for everybody on the day of the move.

17. Several rocks helped provide the truck with stability so it wouldn't slide backward when it was parked.

18. Someone paved most of the roads I drove on to get to the new house.

19. Stacy, the former owner, let me bring over some boxes the day before the move to get a head start on our relocation.
20. My employer paid the cost of the rental truck.
21. Barbara helped pack up my computer.
22. My wife picked up Chinese food for dinner.
23. I received some empty boxes from the local supermarket.
24. Our old Subaru transported some of the more fragile items to the new house.
25. Blankets and pads protected the piano from getting damaged.
26. Our landlady returned our security deposit.

What Did I Give?

1. I gave Ed some money.
2. I gave Dave some money.
3. I paid for lunch and dinner for Ed and Dave.
4. I put gas in the truck.
5. I left the former house relatively clean and in good shape (thanks to my wife).

What Troubles and Difficulties Did I Cause?

1. When I was driving the truck I got stuck at the top of a hill and the cars behind me had to try to get around me. It was getting dark and they couldn't see over the hill, so it was a very dangerous situation. Many of the drivers were delayed and may have been aggravated or even worried about trying to pass me.
2. Ron got out of his car to direct traffic, which put his own safety at risk.

3. We hadn't finished packing, so the whole move took longer than it should have since we had to pack and load the truck at the same time.

4. Lifting all the boxes caused others a lot of sore and tired muscles.

5. I left quite a bit of stuff in my ex-landlady's garage for many weeks, and it created extra difficulty as they were trying to vacate the house for the new owners.

6. My tools got mixed in with tools that were in the rented house, and I believe I may have taken tools that weren't mine.

7. Ron was at the new house longer than expected. His dad was coming from out of town for a visit. He was late getting home and missed dinner. It turned out that his father died a few weeks later and that was the last time he got to see his father.

8. My dog was surely confused and didn't understand what was going on.

9. I put a lot of wear and tear on the truck, its engine, and its tires.

10. I created a lot of confusion because I wasn't sure how to get the piano into the truck.

11. One of the men helping smashed his hand while setting down a large cabinet.

Giving to Others

If you've done the Naikan exercises in the first segment of the book, you've begun to collect information on your debits and credits. Either the world is indebted to you or you are indebted to the world. Of course, there is always a chance that at this point in your life everything has balanced out evenly. When I began examining my life I was surprised at how consistently I had received more than I had given. This seemed to be true whether I was simply reflecting on a single day or on a long-term relationship with a friend or family member. One element of my accounting was grace; I had been cared for and supported far beyond my awareness and expectations. The other element was debt;

> "Forgo forgiving
> for giving."
> MIKE HALL

having given less than I had received, I had to acknowledge the deficit on my life statement.

When we become aware of grace and debt we may naturally wish to give something back to the world. Whether we can actually repay our debt, and avoid increasing it, can only be determined by our sincere effort. The effort itself may lead to the realization that our debt to others can never be repaid. But until we have exhausted ourselves trying, we won't know, nor can we comprehend, the grace that underlies the fabric of our life.

In our efforts to give something back to the world we encounter a great many obstacles. These obstacles include laziness, disorganization, arrogance, selfishness, and pride. We may also have a poor memory, forgetting our past and treating the tasks reality sends us as burdens rather than opportunities for repayment. My friend Gregory Willms and I had been conducting a Naikan retreat, and Gregory was consistently doing much more than his share of washing dishes. I returned from the supermarket one afternoon to find him once again laboring over the kitchen sink.

"Why don't you leave those, Gregory. I'll get to them as soon as I put away the groceries," I said.

"It's all right. When I consider how many of my dirty dishes have been washed by others, I'll never be able to do enough dishes to even it out."

Gregory had transcended the smaller perspective of seeing only the dishes washed over the course of a few days in comparison with his colleagues. Had this been the direction of his awareness he might have resented washing another full sink of dishes. But by being aware of the totality of all the dishes that had been washed for him, he encountered dirty dishes as simply an opportunity to make a small payment back to the world. It was not a big deal. It was simply service with nothing extra added.

Compassion and Attention

Is it possible to act compassionately if our attention is on ourselves? When our attention is focused outward we notice opportunities to give to others. But when our attention is focused inward on our discomfort, anger, inconvenience, or desires, then such opportunities go unnoticed. The qualities of outward attention and compassion are so intermingled that it is difficult to imagine a person possessing the latter quality without the former.

There is a story in which an assassin arrives at one of Gandhi's public speeches, concealing a gun and intending to kill him. After hearing Gandhi address the crowd, the man is moved to tears. He drops his weapon and runs up to where Gandhi is standing. As he falls to his knees he confesses in shame that he was sent to assassinate Gandhi but cannot carry out his assignment. Gandhi's response is to ask *what will happen to him for failing to carry out the assassination.* Imagine having just been told that you were about to be killed, that only moments ago a man with a gun was about to put a bullet through your head and end your life. Yet Gandhi's concern is for

> "Have a look at the apple tree in your yard. Look at it with complete attention. It is truly a miracle. If you notice it, you will take good care of it, and you too are part of its miraculousness."
> THICH NHAT HANH

the man's predicament, not his own. "What will happen to you?" he asks. "What kind of trouble will you be in?" It seems inconceivable that having unintentionally persuaded an assassin not to kill me, I could be concerned about the trouble I have caused the assassin. Yet that was Gandhi's sentiment.

Gandhi's perspective echoes Naikan's third question, "What trouble am I causing others?" Can you think of a more perfectly compassionate response? Notice the focus of his attention. It is not on his own fear or anxiety, nor does he respond with concern for his own well-being. His attention is on others.

William James cites the case of author Horace Fletcher. Having checked out of his hotel, he was waiting at the train station to board a train, but his bags had not yet arrived from the hotel. As the train pulled away, the hotel porter arrived gasping for breath and carrying Mr. Fletcher's bags. He looked as if he feared a scolding. Fletcher related: "I said to him, 'It doesn't matter at all, you couldn't help it, so we will try again tomorrow. Here is your fee, I am sorry you had all this trouble earning it.' The look of surprise that came over his face was so filled with pleasure that I was paid on the spot for the delay in my departure. The next day he would not accept a cent for the service, and he and I are friends for life."

Where is Fletcher's attention? He notices the porter's effort and discomfort and he imagines how disappointed the porter must feel having not made it to the train with the bags on time. Fletcher pays him and then Fletcher apologizes to the porter!

Both Gandhi and Fletcher are more concerned about the suffering they are causing others than about the suffering others are causing them. Their attention to others allows them to notice the suffering and problems of others and, consequently, they are able to act compassionately.

Perhaps these stories are extraordinary. Perhaps they are just a natural response to the shift in attention that self-reflection can inspire. We can open our eyes. We can begin asking a different question. Instead of the question "How can others be of use to me?" we can ask, "How can I be of use to others?"

Strategies for Giving Yourself Away

In the 1940s David Dunn wrote a brief article for *Forbes Magazine* entitled, "Try Giving Yourself Away." It was reprinted in *Reader's Digest* and was subsequently expanded and published as a book in 1947. Dunn states that he adopted "giving himself away" as a hobby, not because he wished to be unselfish, generous, or self-sac-rificing, but because he found that such a hobby enriched his life immensely. Here is a summary of his strategies and suggestions for those who also wish to take up this hobby:

- Pass on helpful ideas to others. If you go into a store and think of an idea that might benefit the store, mention it to the store manager or write a brief letter.
- Thank waiters for good service and chefs for tasty meals.
- Rather than giving money, give your time and effort to others.
- Obey your giving impulses and act quickly when a situation presents itself.

> **"It seems to be a law of life that we enrich ourselves most when we give ourselves most fully and freely."**
> **DAVID DUNN**

- Start giving yourself away as early in the morning as possible.
- You don't need a lot of extra time—even minutes a day will make a difference.
- To discover new opportunities for giving yourself away, put yourself in the shoes of every person you encounter.
- A smile is one thing that transcends any language barrier. Smile often.
- Send letters and postcards daily.
- Leave a trail of appreciation behind you.
- Be specific when you thank and compliment others.
- Cultivate the habit of noticing things and becoming more alert to the world around you.
- Pick up garbage and debris on the road.

Dunn suggests we not confine our giving away too narrowly but create an ever-widening circle of recipients. He states:

> The most important reason for not concentrating our giving-away on a few people is that it tends to make them selfish, which is as great a disservice as one human being can do to others. . . . So, when people grow used to your gifts of yourself and begin to demand them, it is time to stop giving so much to those particular people.

So as you reflect on your life and are inspired to give something back to the world, try some of Dunn's suggestions. The awareness that comes from reflection and the actions of giving will often stimulate one another. And as we give we continue to receive. We receive in order to give; we receive as a result of giving. We pay off our debt and watch it grow.

Giving away. Giving—*A Way*.

Service Is Attention

A secret service is a service that is done for someone while the service provider's identity remains a secret. The one who serves receives no credit or acknowledgment. At a Constructive Living training program, one of the participants was given the assignment of doing a secret service for another participant. After two days she still hadn't done anything. She explained how frustrated and embarrassed she felt and that she just couldn't think of any secret service she could perform. That afternoon she went to the supermarket with me. When we arrived I asked her to stay outside. "Look at this store," I said, "please look at it closely. See if you can think of three secret services you could do for this store. I'll go in and get the groceries." When I returned in about twenty minutes she casually listed three secret services she could do for the store:

- Picking up the litter in the parking lot
- Taking an old, outdated poster off the wall
- Bringing the stray grocery carts to the front of the store

She realized that she had been completely absorbed in her internal experience of trying to think of something to do. Then she turned her attention even further inward and focused on the frustration and embarrassment that followed. She did her assignment as soon as we returned.

When we shift our attention to the reality around us, to our spouse, our car, the service station attendant, we see countless opportunities to care for others. But those who are most preoccupied with themselves suffer the most. They also fail to experience the satisfaction of attending to the needs of another.

If we turn our attention to the world often enough, we may notice that we are truly incapable of even a compassionate act without the consistent and concrete support of others. We feed the birds with birdseed provided by others. We help a frustrated driver change a tire with tools and a tire manufactured by others. We make a contribution to a relief agency with money given to us by others. We are simply members of a very large team assembled to meet life's needs at any given moment. The team works well. In fact, it works so well that it's difficult to identify any particular player. Each seems to possess elements borrowed from the others.

Reconstructing Reality

I spent the other day at the Sweet Onion Inn in Hancock, Vermont, doing construction work. My friend Ron, the owner of the inn, is building a house for his family next door and I went down to help him. I do this as a "favor" to him and he also comes up to the TōDō Institute and helps with repairs and renovations in a similar way. It's a nice arrangement and it's easy for me to think of this barter situation as a "wash." I help him, he helps me.

But even after a few minutes of self-reflection I realize it's not a wash at all. Ron has been here many more times than I have been there. It's a two-hour drive round-trip, and that means he's put in a lot more driving time as well. When the TōDō Institute first bought this property, there was a septic problem one week after we moved in. It turned out that we had to dig up the septic tank and replace the pipe running from the house to the tank. Unfortunately, this pipe ran directly underneath a beautiful wood deck from which you can see the sunset over the Adirondack Mountains. For several days Ron came out and painstakingly helped me tear the deck apart so a backhoe could dig up the ground. It was November and there was snow on the ground and the deck was frozen, so he brought portable propane heaters that were placed under the deck to unfreeze the wood.

He helped us renovate the office and build a future bedroom for my adopted daughter before she arrived from China. He helped me turn a wooden desktop into a diaper-changing table. He helped me install a bath/shower in the basement. When my daughter arrived from China, he brought her a welcome gift, a small rocking chair that he had made himself.

Before moving to Vermont, Ron was a professional builder and carpenter. When he comes here he brings tools for us to use that I didn't know existed. When I go there I bring a hammer and a screwdriver. When he works here I function as an assistant. When I go there I also function as an assistant.

When we're doing a "favor" for someone, it's easy to develop a sense of pride or think, "How nice a person I am to be doing this." But in some cases, when we see how much we received from somebody in the past, we are humbled and realize that this is only an opportunity to pay back a small sum toward a much greater wealth of gifts and services that have been given to us. This is an important consideration when we find ourselves taking care of our older parents. How easy it is to forget the years in which they changed our diapers and bathed us.

While doing my favor for Ron, I received some expert tips on how to use special handles to carry wallboard, how to use a hammer-type staple gun, how to match angles when installing a stair-case, and, as a fringe benefit, I was given a homemade scone, an oatmeal cookie, a cup of tea, and a piece of bean pie that was being made for dinner guests.

When I got home later that evening, I walked through a brand-new steel, insulated front door that Ron had helped me install the previous Tuesday. Hinges allow that door to open and close with ease. My realistic humility hinges on my ability to remember what was done for me in the past.

Don't Thank Me . . .

Carl is an old, white-haired man who lives in a small town in the Green Mountains of Vermont. He wears a green cap and drives a rusted, gray pickup truck.

Carl's a friendly, likable sort of fellow. He doesn't talk much but he'll always wave to you on a country road, even if he doesn't know you. He's the kind of guy that will stop and help you fix a flat tire on a Sunday morning, even though it makes him late for church. He figures, "why sit in church listening to someone talk about God when you could be out here working for him?"

One strange thing about Carl is that whenever you thank him for something, he won't take any credit. Instead, he passes on the credit to someone, or something else. For example, he dropped off a 20-lb. bag of potatoes at Mrs. Archer's and she thanked him. He said, "Don't thank me, thank the potatoes."

On another occasion he helped John Stevens fix his tractor. When John thanked him, Carl said, "Don't thank me, thank my dad. He's the one who taught me everything I know about tractors."

When Beth Wilder thanked Carl for dropping her off in town one icy, winter morning, he said, "Don't thank me, thank my truck."

People who know Carl have become accustomed to this amusing little eccentricity in his speech. Sometimes the kids will even look for opportunities to thank him for something, just to hear a creative "Don't thank me." In fact, they've made it into a kind of game.

When five-year-old Jessica made her mom a birthday card, her mom gave her a hug and thanked her. Jessica smiled at her and said, "Don't thank me, thank the crayons." Well, her mom laughed so hard she was rolling on the floor.

A few years back, somebody asked Carl why he talked this way: "Why do you always say, 'Don't thank me,' and then pass on the thanks to someone or something else?"

Carl paused for a moment and thought. "Well," he said, "That's just how it is."

Thanks, Carl.

A Fable: The Giving Princess

Long ago in the far-off land of Imperfexshun lived a princess named Lynea. She was very beautiful, and ever since she was a child her heart was filled with kindness. She therefore decided that she wanted to dedicate her life to being kind and compassionate to all beings. Part of her effort involved the giving of gifts whenever possible.

As time passed and her dedication to this giving way of life became stronger, a problem surfaced. It seemed that the more she dedicated herself to giving, the more she became obsessed with giving the "perfect" gifts. Finally it reached the point where she would not give a single gift; for every gift she considered had some minor imperfection. It was for this reason that she went to see Merlin, a magician of great power and reputation throughout the land.

"Lately, things have become so bad that I cannot give a single gift in any situation. I will give you three examples. First there was an old beggar who came to the castle on the coldest day of the winter. It was so cold that I dared not go outside for I would instantly freeze. The beggar, who was cold and distraught, asked if she might have an old winter coat that would help keep him warm. Now I have many winter coats, but none would be adequate in such devastating weather. One coat had fur, but it had no hood. Another coat had a hood but no lining. Knowing that no coat would suffice, I returned empty-handed and expressed my sincere regrets. My heart was filled with sadness for him, but I could not bring myself to give him a coat that would not perfectly meet his needs.

"On a second occasion, I decided to give my father a painting for his birthday. I went to his favorite stream in the woods and set up my canvas and began to paint. Unfortunately, I am a painter of only modest skills, and, try as I might, I could not capture the beauty of that stream, running through the forest, on my canvas. Canvas after canvas I would discard because it was not good enough. Finally, my father's birthday came and went and I had no gift for him. Once again my heart was filled with sadness and regret.

"And finally, last week I was married to a handsome young man from a nearby kingdom. I love him very much and I wished to make our wedding night a very special one. But when it was time to go to bed, I found that I could not disrobe. Knowing the imperfections of my own body, I was ashamed to offer him such a gift from his bride. Thus it has come to pass that we have not yet consummated our marriage. This causes him great distress, and once again my heart is filled with sadness.

"I have come to you, Merlin, because you have great magical powers and I would ask that you cast a magic spell so that all my gifts may be perfect ones and I shall no longer have any reason to withhold them."

Merlin looked deeply into the princess's eyes. He could see the pain and suffering that she had borne. But, alas, when he finally spoke, he had no magic to offer her."

I am sorry my princess, but I know of no spell that will grant your wish. I can see that you suffer very much, for though your heart is filled with kindness, it is the act of giving that makes one a kind person. And though your thoughts are filled with compassion, it is the act of caring that makes one a compassionate person. It is clear that unless you can solve this problem, your life's purpose will surely be sacrificed."

And at that moment the princess began to cry, because she could not bear to live a life without giving.

"I do have one suggestion that might help, however. Come back in three days, and bring with you three warm coats and three good paintings."

So the princess, still in tears, went back to the castle and gathered her three warmest coats and her three best canvases, though she was still not perfectly happy with any of them. When she returned, Merlin asked her which was the warmest of the three coats. She examined each closely, explaining its imperfections, but finally chose a large brown coat as the best. Next he asked her which was the best of the three paintings. This was more difficult, and she took a great deal of time going back and forth between them. She finally settled on one particular painting while taking great pains to explain its shortcomings.

Then Merlin spoke: "Now here is what you are to do. Take the coat you have selected and give it to the old beggar as a gift. Then take the painting you have selected and give it to your father for his birthday. If your mind fills itself with thoughts of imperfection, simply accept such thoughts and give the gifts anyway. When you have completed this assignment, return here."

The princess began to protest, but Merlin would have none of that and quickly ushered her out.

On her way back to the castle, she was surprised to find the beggar, haggard and thin, roaming through the streets asking for food and money. She approached him with reservation, glancing at the coat she held. "Pardon me old man, but I recognize you from an earlier meeting at the castle. At that time I failed to provide you with an adequate coat as you requested, for I had none that would suffice. Though the situation remains unchanged, I would now offer you this coat I carry with me, but I must be truthful in telling you that on the coldest of winter days it will fail to keep you warm. Still, it is yours if you will accept it."

The beggar put on the coat and immediately felt its warmth. He knelt before the princess in gratitude and told her that the coat was the nicest gift he had ever received. He continued to thank her and, even as she departed from his company, he sang her praises to all who passed by.

When she arrived at the castle she went directly to her father's chambers. "My dear father," she said, "forgive me for failing to present you with a birthday gift this past year. I labored intensely to create a painting of your favorite stream in the woods, yet I could not succeed in capturing the beauty of such a setting. Instead, I must present you with the imperfect product of my toil and hope that you will pardon the limits of my craft." She then presented her father with the painting she had selected, and to her surprise he was overcome with joy. "This is the loveliest present I have ever received and well worth waiting for. I shall truly cherish it as long as I shall live."

The princess was pleased, and somewhat surprised, that her gifts had brought so much joy to their recipients. The next morning she hurried back to Merlin to tell him of the news. But at the end of her tale, her eyes, once again, turned to despair as she considered the predicament of her husband. "I fear that in this case your advice is of no use. I have but one body and no alternatives to choose from. Yet my concerns regarding its imperfections have not diminished. Please, Merlin, there must be some magic spell to help me."

Merlin thought for a moment, and then leaned back in his chair. "How nice that you only have one body, for you will not have to suffer the agony of choosing. Your desire to offer your husband that which is perfect comes from your desire to please him and make him happy. Even if I did have a magic potion that would relieve you of your anxiety, I would not use it for fear of relieving you also of your love for your husband. The anxiety and the love are simply two sides of the same coin. I will, however, give you this advice: Accept your fear, anxiety, and concerns about this gift and consummate your marriage anyway. Your worries have no real power over you. Like the clouds in the sky, they come and go but they do not prevent the grass from growing."

The princess was confused, but that night, amidst her worries and concerns, she and her husband made love, and she had little attention remaining for worries of imperfection.

The next day she returned and told Merlin of her experience (not in detail, of course). She said, "My dear magician, you have been so helpful to me that I would like to try to repay you for your kindness and wisdom. I am a princess and there is great wealth and rich treasures at my disposal. You may have anything in the kingdom you desire. Please tell me how I may repay you."

"I have only one request," said Merlin. "Please bring me a gift that is truly yours to give."

"I don't understand," said the princess. "What do you mean by a gift that is truly mine to give?"

But Merlin had already left the room.

For many days the princess pondered his request. She made a list of all her treasures and possessions. She thought about each item; from whom it had come, of what it was made, when it was given to her. She considered her paintings, her hair, even some fables she had written for children. But in her reflection she could find nothing that would meet Merlin's request. For a while she felt sad, even impoverished. Of all her treasures and possessions, not one was truly hers. She locked herself in her room for several days and refused to talk to anyone. Her family and many people in the kingdom became worried about her.

Then one day she emerged from her room. She looked surprisingly well. There was a gentle quality to her voice, and her eyes appeared to be softer. She apologized to her family for her long absence, but said nothing of her experience. She began going about her daily work once more.

In the ages to come she was remembered for her kindness and wisdom, and many stories were told about her life. Yet none could ever explain what happened to her while she was in her room. After Merlin died, they found a note in his desk written, apparently, in the princess's hand. It said,

In looking for something
I found Nothing.
And in Nothing I found everything.

In poverty I found riches.
And in silence, music.

Abdicating my goodness, abandoning my efforts
in imperfection, perfection.

A Moral Self-Examination

There is an element of our human nature that is poised to judge the conduct of others as soon as that conduct falls short of our ideals. This is particularly true when their conduct causes problems or difficulties for us. How could she do such a thing? How could he treat me like that? How dare he lie to me! How dare she steal! We do not hesitate to provide punishment—in words and deeds—when others transgress against us. And even when we forgive, we do it from a pedestal.

But what of our own transgres-

> "We have thrown down a light burden, which is the reprehending of our own selves, and we have chosen instead to bear a heavy burden, by justifying our own selves and condemning others."
>
> ABBOT JOHN, FROM *THE WISDOM OF THE DESERT*

sions? How often do we examine our responsibility for the pain of others? How often do we see our own culpability in an argument? How often do we reflect on our own misconduct with the same energy and effort with which we criticize the behavior of others? We seem to have developed a skill for dismissing and excusing ourselves, even as we accuse others who have acted no less virtuously. As Bishop Fulton J. Sheen states,

> We wrong others and deny there is any guilt; others do the same to us, and we say that they should have known better. . . . We flatter others because of what they can do for us and call it "love"; we lie to them, and call it "tact.". . . We overeat and call it "health"; we pile up more wealth than is necessary for our state in life and call it "security.". . . We begin sentences with "I" and condemn our neighbor as a bore for wanting to talk about himself, when we want to talk about ourselves.

We are a species skilled in the art of self-deception. In the interest of a glowing self-image and high self-esteem, we have sacrificed something much more important: truth. If we venture into the arena of self-reflection, we might discover that our reality does not match the image we hold of ourselves. Then we will have to give up one or the other.

Conducting a sincere and honest examination of our lives is a challenging task. It is particularly challenging when we must face incidents and events of our past in which our behavior was hurtful to others. But if we limit our reflection to only those moments of pleasure, accomplishment, and kindness, we fail to develop an accurate portrait of our existence. The discovery and examination of our innate selfishness transforms love from that which is deserved to that which is a gift. As long as we deny and dismiss this aspect of our nature, we cannot come to this realization.

We are frightened of giving up our illusions about ourselves, yet, in reality, it is not a dangerous journey. It is the safest method of travel. The trip itself gives us direction and purpose. The further we go, the stronger our faith.

With each step,
shoes, crafted by others,
protect and comfort my feet.

Benjamin Franklin

We generally remember Benjamin Franklin as a diplomat, politician, and scientist, but it is likely that his emphasis on self-reflection accounted for his greatness in many of these areas. He designed a rather systematic approach to self-reflection that preceded Naikan by almost two hundred years. Franklin's method of reflecting on violations of a predetermined set of moral standards resembles, in spirit and practice, the third question in Naikan reflection.

At first his efforts were limited to personal conviction and casual application, but he quickly saw the difficulty of attempting to build character and healthy life habits without some formal method of self-evaluation and reflection:

> While my attention was taken up and care employed in guarding against one fault, I was often surprised by another. Habit took the advantage of inattention. Inclination was sometimes too strong
>
> for reason. I concluded at length that the mere speculative con-

viction that it was in our interest to be completely virtuous was not sufficient to prevent slipping, and that the contrary habits must be broken and good ones acquired before we can have any dependence on a steady, uniform rectitude of conduct.

Franklin's method of self-examination began with the identification of twelve virtues against which he desired to evaluate his conduct:

1. **Temperance:** Eat not to dullness. Drink not to elevation.
2. **Silence:** Speak not but what may benefit others or yourself. Avoid trifling conversation.
3. **Order:** Let all your things have their places. Let each part of your business have its time.
4. **Resolution:** Resolve to perform what you ought. Perform without fail what you resolve.
5. **Frugality:** Make no expense but to do good to others or yourself; waste nothing.
6. **Lose No Time [Industry]:** Be always employed in something useful. Cut off all unnecessary actions.
7. **Sincerity:** Use no hurtful deceit. Think innocently and justly; and, if you speak, speak accordingly.
8. **Justice:** Wrong none by doing injuries or omitting the benefits that are your duty.
9. **Moderation:** Avoid extremes. Forbear resenting injuries so much as you think they deserve.
10. **Cleanliness:** Tolerate no uncleanliness in body, clothes, or habitation.
11. **Tranquility:** Be not disturbed at trifles or at accidents common or unavoidable.
12. **Chastity:** Rarely use venery but for health or offspring—

never to dullness, weakness, or the injury of your own or another's peace or reputation.

Franklin states that he purposely avoided adoption of the tenets of any particular religion or sect. Though it incorporated some of his own religious and moral beliefs, he wished his method to be usable by people of all religions.

After developing his list of twelve virtues, he added a thirteenth, humility. It seems that a Quaker friend of his convinced him that pride was one of his most apparent traits, regularly revealing itself in conversations where Franklin was overbearing and even arrogant in arguing his point. Being convinced of the truth of his friend's observation, Franklin added humility to his list with a determination to rid himself of pride, along with his other vices.

Franklin designed a little book for himself, allotting one page for each of the thirteen virtues. He set up a grid in which the days of the week appeared at the top of the grid and the thirteen virtues were listed vertically along the left side by their first initial (see the chart on facing page).

Each week he concentrated on only one virtue, leaving the others to chance. At the end of the day, he reflected on his conduct and placed a check mark alongside the appropriate virtue if he found he had committed an offense against his moral ideal. At the end of the week, his checks, and their absence, provided a picture of his conduct in relation to the selected virtue for that week.

If in the first week I could keep my first line clear of spots [checks], I supposed the habit of that virtue so much strengthened and its opposite weakened that I might venture extending my attention to include the next, and for the following week

	Sun.	Mon.	Tues.	Wed.	Thurs.	Fri.	Sat.
Temperance							
Silence							
Order							
Resolution							
Frugality							
Industry							
Sincerity							
Justice							
Moderation							
Cleanliness							
Tranquility							
Chastity							
Humility							

keep both lines clear of spots. And like him who, having a garden to weed, does not attempt to eradicate all the bad herbs at once, which would exceed his reach and his strength, but works on one of the beds at a time, and having accomplished the first, proceeds to a second; so I should have (I hoped) the encouraging pleasure of seeing on my pages the progress I made in virtue by clearing successively my lines of their spots, till in the end by a number of courses, I should be happy in viewing a clean book after a thirteen weeks' daily examination.

After thirteen weeks, Franklin began the entire process again, making it possible to run through his entire course four times in a year.

And how did he fare? He was surprised to see himself with so many faults, though he states that they did diminish somewhat over time. With regard to time, he found it difficult to establish a routine schedule due, in part, to the constant and unpredictable arrival of visitors. With regard to the order of his possessions, his lack of progress caused him even greater frustration. He stated:

> My faults in it [i.e., Order] vexed me so much, and I made so little progress in amendment and have such frequent relapses, that I was almost ready to give up the attempt and content myself with a faulty character in that respect. In truth, I found myself incorrigible with respect to Order; and now I am old and my memory bad, I feel very sensibly the want of it.

Another virtue with which he struggled was humility. He says that he had little success acquiring the realization of this virtue, though he made some progress in creating the appearance of it:

> In reality there is perhaps no one of our natural passions so hard to subdue as Pride; disguise it, struggle with it, beat it down, stifle it, mortify it as much as one pleases, it is still alive and will every now and then peep out and show itself. . . . For even if I could conceive that I had completely overcome it, I should probably be proud of my humility.

The number of years in which Franklin employed his system of self-reflection is not clear. In successive years he would scratch out the old check marks to make room for new ones as he examined his conduct over and over. The scratch marks eventually became holes, and he would start a new book. Even when he ceased to use his system formally, he always carried his little book with him.

His system, and his experience using it, resembles that of a Japanese samurai, Tsunetomo Yamamoto, who died while Franklin was still a child. Yamamoto writes:

When I was young, I kept a "Diary of Regret" and tried to record my mistakes day by day, but there was never a day when I didn't have twenty or thirty entries. As there was no end to it, I gave up. Even today, when I think about the day's affairs after going to bed, there is never a day when I do not make some blunder in speaking or in some activity. Living without mistakes is truly impossible. But this is something that people who live by cleverness have no inclination to think about.

Though sincere and persistent, it appears that Franklin never mastered his entire list of virtues. Yet his efforts to continually examine his life were of great importance. What is revealed through the process of self-reflection? What do we learn? How do we change, yet remain the same?

Though I never arrived at the perfection I had been so ambitious of obtaining but fell far short of it, yet I was by the endeavor a better and a happier man than I otherwise should have been if I had not attempted it; as those who aim at perfect writing by imitating the engraved copies, tho' they never reach the wished-for excellence of those copies, their hand is mended by the endeavor and is tolerable while it continues fair and legible.

Benjamin Franklin died in Philadelphia in 1790. Thank you, Mr. Franklin. You left us a great deal.

The Troubles We Cause

Ishin Yoshimoto's method of self-reflection differed from Franklin's in several respects. The first two questions in Naikan ask us to reflect on the give-and-take nature of our lives, so we become more accurately aware of the support we give to others and the support we receive from others. The third question in Naikan asks us to consider the troubles and difficulties we have caused others. Yoshimoto undoubtedly considered this an important task, as he asked those who were reflecting to dedicate a minimum of 60 percent of their time to this question alone. Unlike Franklin's method, there is no predetermined set of moral standards against which we measure our conduct. Instead, we are simply considering ways in which our conduct caused trouble, harm, difficulty, suffering, or inconvenience to others. For actions that can indeed be characterized this way, we are not necessarily acknowledging that such actions were "wrong," "bad," or "immoral."

In some cases, we may find that conduct such as helping a victim of a car accident causes "inconvenience" to someone who is waiting for us at a restaurant. Yet we would probably not characterize our offer of assistance as wrong or immoral. Yet in other cases involving conduct such as a sarcastic comment, an untruthful excuse, or a forgotten responsibility, we may well decide that what we did was selfish, wrong, or immoral. However, the third question of Naikan is basically concerned with whether your conduct caused problems to others. This is a simple standard, certainly less complex than deducing whether one's actions were bad or good.

> "We know so many things, but we don't know ourselves! Why, thirty or forty skins or hides, as thick and hard as an ox's or a bear's, cover the soul. Go into your own ground and learn to know yourself there."
>
> MEISTER ECKHART

We may struggle to understand how we cause trouble to others because we may be so often preoccupied with our own comfort and convenience that we fail to see how our actions are impacting others. A few years ago I was flying back to the United States from Hong Kong. I was sitting next to a lovely young woman who was a nurse. We exchanged some information about our jobs, and the topic of self-reflection came up. As I was trying to concisely explain Naikan to her, I found my attention shifting, from time to time, to the irritation I felt at the cramped seats, particularly the violation of my "eating space" caused by the person in front of me, who had so inconsiderately reclined his chair all the way back while I was in the middle of my dinner. In fact, I was about to use this as a perfect example of how we don't pay attention to the troubles we cause, when I paused for a moment to consider the position of my own seat, which I had reclined as soon as I completed my meal. I carefully glanced behind me to find an older gentleman not more than halfway through his meal. So while I was poised to point the finger at the

"If we do something good when no one is looking, we wish to be praised or recognized, and we go around telling people what we have done. If we are not appreciated or are slandered, we are disappointed and feel that what we have done is less worthwhile. When we have done something bad, we are afraid that others may find out, and so we try our best to hide it. If we have managed to hide it, we feel we have gained something . . . [but] the fact of our action remains a fact, which will eternally make up one page in our life, serving as either a positive or negative factor in the formation of our character . . . it becomes a karmic force that accompanies us."
REV. SHUNDO AOYAMA

person in front of me, I was doing the same thing to the person behind me.

It's very hard to truly put yourself in another person's shoes, to try to imagine what it would be like to be that person. And furthermore, to imagine being the other person and having to deal with someone like you! Our minds and hearts are not well versed in this skill. We are very good at putting ourselves in our own shoes and noticing what it is like to deal with everybody else. But it takes a profound shift of awareness to temporarily abandon our personal perspective and consider the perspective of another being.

So when we cause problems or inconvenience to someone, it is not enough to merely notice the problem or even offer a mindless "sorry about that." If we are truly committed to a sincere and honest examination of our conduct, we must go further and try to understand the other person's experience. Parents often have greater anxiety about the safety of their children than the children do over the safety of their parents. So if you are a teenage girl and you come home three hours past your expected time of return, you must try to consider the worry you have caused your parents by reflecting on it from their point of view. Conversely, a parent whose daughter is married and has a family may make critical comments about her husband and his behavior. The parent may consider such comments as relatively harmless, but it is important to consider these comments from the viewpoint of the daughter and her husband. When our perspective changes, even momentarily, we are more likely to attain a realistic understanding of other people and how our conduct is affecting them.

Through the third question we come to realize that we cannot observe ourselves directly, just as the eye cannot see itself. We need a mirror. And that mirror is the experience of others with whom we make contact. Through their eyes and heart we discover a path to self-awareness.

Lying and Stealing

Naikan self-reflection involves the examination of our relationships with others. One element of this relationship is how we have caused troubles and difficulties. Another element of Naikan self-reflection involves the examination of how we have lied and stolen from others. We can examine such behavior over the course of a single day, or year by year, until we have covered our entire life. Why would we want to do such a thing? Wouldn't this just make us feel bad?

Of course, we may not be pleased with our conduct when we have lied or stolen. We may feel remorse, shame, or guilt. But if we do, isn't this a healthy response to such behavior? Guilt or remorse may not feel good, but they remind us that our behavior

"Then came the day when we were asked to consider our history of lying, stealing, and cheating. By the time I had reached the period of reflecting on my adolescence, I realized that for the first time in my life I was actually facing myself and the numerous transgressions that I had committed in my life. It dawned on me that for forty years I had attended services on the Jewish High Holidays and when it was time on Yom Kippur, the Day of Atonement, to confess my sins with the rest of the community, I always thought that those words in the prayer book were for someone else's wrongdoings. Me arrogant, bigoted, cynical? Me deceitful, egotistical, greedy, jealous? It must be others who were obstinate, possessive, rancorous, selfish. They were the ones who yielded to temptation, were lustful or malicious. And in that moment I saw myself for who I had been, for what I had done, for the many I had hurt and disrespected, for a litany of wrongdoings. For years of stealing, lying, and cheating. And so I requested that I not be brought food, that in the tradition of my religion I fast, that I purify myself, that I begin to become clean. My life until that day had been a 'Grand Illusion' and it was time to look into the corners of my memory and acknowledge the misdeeds of my life."

BARBARA SARAH

has consequences for others. For the recovering alcoholic, it is unpleasant to recall how drinking has caused suffering for his family and friends. But it is very dangerous to forget such experiences.

The majority of people who attend a Naikan retreat at our center in Vermont report that it was the reflection on their lying and stealing, over the course of their entire life, that was the most meaningful or profound aspect of their experience. We travel through our personal history searching for our transgressions and harm that we have caused others. Of course, we can avoid such a journey. But our unwillingness to see the facts of our life does not change the facts of our life.

The Senkobo Naikan Center in Japan provides the following guidelines, which were originally developed by the Reverend Shue Usami, for reflecting on how we have lied or stolen. I have modified them slightly for use by Westerners.

Lying

1. Have we told others something that was not completely truthful?

2. Have we failed to keep promises, commitments, appointments, or vows?

3. Have we acted in ways that have caused others to lose confidence or trust in us?

4. Have we misled or deceived others? Knowing that others held certain assumptions that were not true, did we allow them to go on believing their false assumptions rather than provide the truth?

5. Did we sell, trade, or exchange something we knew to be defective or deficient without revealing such information to others?

6. Have we acted in ways that caused us to lose credit or the financial trust of others?

Stealing

1. Have we looked at something or seen things that were not meant for us to see?

2. Have we eavesdropped or overheard something that was not proper for us to hear?

3. Have we taken things and objects that did not belong to us? In what ways have we stolen from our parents and other family members? What have we stolen from others who supported us?

4. Other than objects and things, what else have we taken that did not belong to us?

5. Have we stolen the time of others?

An Appeal on Behalf of Guilt

Perhaps guilt has not received a fair trial. Perhaps, after all these years, we shall discover that we have misjudged guilt, as in the case of the convicted felon who is exonerated from his crime when new evidence arises to prove his innocence. And if his release from unjust incarceration causes us to feel guilty for the suffering we have caused, what greater evidence can there be to refute the original conviction?

We cannot defend guilt from the accusation that it is not enjoyable. If "feeling good" is the test, then there is no need for a retrial. But the right combination of drugs can help us to feel good most of the time, and yet few of us would advocate such an approach to life. For those who see a purpose to life beyond that of feeling good, then we would be wise to reconsider the matter of guilt.

Guilt is relevant because it is a likely outcome of any effort to examine our lives. If we reflect on how we have lived, we are likely to see occasions when we have caused harm or suffering to others. Such awareness may stimulate the feelings and thoughts that we commonly refer to as "guilt." If we look beneath these feelings, what might we find?

If we judge our behavior to have been wrong, immoral, or unethical, then guilt is simply a messenger bringing a piece of news to our attention. To try to cure ourselves of guilt is like hospitalizing the messenger who brings news of another's illness. Our problem is not guilt. Our problem is what we have done or how we are living. We must treat the

> **"Must I hold a candle to my shames?"**
> JESSICA, IN *THE MERCHANT OF VENICE*

patient directly. To seek for, or receive, reassurance that "we should not feel guilty" from a friend or therapist is to deny our own experience. Such comfort may actually harm us by shifting our attention toward the symptom (how we are feeling) and away from the problem (how we are living).

Guilt may also arise from a debt that we recognize. If we review the balance between what we have received and what we have given in any particular relationship, we may feel guilty if we discover that we are in debt. If I borrow money from you and repay only half the original amount, I will see, upon reflection, that I still owe the remaining half. If I do not repay this amount, it is quite natural for me to feel guilty. If I have not even attempted repayment, or if I find that it is virtually impossible for me to repay my debt even though I wish to repay it, then guilt may arise. In these cases my guilt arises because I recognize that I have received more from you than I have given in return. Gratitude may arise as well. Nobody tries to cure us of gratitude. Perhaps it is because gratitude feels good. But guilt and gratitude may have more in common than we realize.

Let us also consider the relationship between guilt and compassion. Suppose your friend lends you his car because your car is being repaired. At the end of the day you are returning the car, when you notice that it has a scratch on the door that wasn't there before. You feel terribly guilty about the scratch. Isn't it possible that the source of your guilt is the same as the source of your concern for your friend? If you did not care about your friend, would you feel guilty? The Japanese psychiatrist Shoma Morita would often refer to fear of death and the desire to live as "two sides of the same coin." And so compassion may be the other side of the coin of guilt. To see the relationship between guilt and compassion may teach us it is all right to feel guilty. We do not need to fix our guilt. Rather than talk about or work through our guilt, it would be more constructive to repair the scratch.

But suppose when this incident occurred we deceived our friend, and now it's too late to repair the scratch. We still feel guilty. What can we do? Perhaps we can tell our friend the truth now. Perhaps some other form of restitution is possible. But even restitution doesn't change the past; it only creates a new present. There will always be limits to our own self-willed efforts to live a better life. C. S. Lewis raises the issue when he says,

> The moral law may exist to be transcended: but there is no transcending it for those who have not first admitted its claims upon them, and then tried with all their strength to meet that claim, and fairly and squarely faced the fact of their failure.

So is the absence of guilt an indication of enlightened living, or is it a symptom of self-deception?

Guilt is not really the issue. If guilt ends up distracting us from reality, shall we blame guilt rather than ourselves? I would like to file an appeal on behalf of guilt. Let's review the actual record. Let's hold a hearing to consider the innocence of guilt. I vote for acquittal, for freedom. Let guilt come and go as it pleases. Let's find the real perpetrator and put him on trial. As punishment for his crimes, he'll be sentenced to a life of grace. That will teach him a lesson.

Apologies

Recently a woman I had dated for several years got married. She was kind enough to invite me to her wedding. It was a lovely ceremony, and afterward there was the traditional reception line. I shook hands with her parents and congratulated them. I also handed them an envelope. It was not a gift, but a letter of apology. I apologized for the difficulties I had caused them during the time I was their daughter's boyfriend. It was a note that I could have, and should have, written while I was still dating their daughter. But I hadn't. My attention had always been focused on the difficulties they had caused me.

When I sat down to write that note, I reflected exclusively on the trouble and difficulty I had caused them. I had created great anguish by encouraging my girlfriend to insist that we share a room when visiting her parents for the holidays. I had disturbed the harmony of holiday dinners by raising controversial questions of politics, religion, and vegetarianism. I had spoken critically of their lifestyle to others, because I did not approve of many of their values. I think it was the first time I had experienced remorse for my own behavior during those years. It was also the first time I reflected on my relationship with them, judging my own actions and not theirs. By eliminating the question of right versus wrong from consideration, a space was created in which I could more clearly see the problems I had caused them.

Why do we have so much trouble offering a genuine apology to another human being? Why does our mind seem to offer such resistance? How easy it is to condemn and judge the behavior of others. Even if we do not voice such judgments, we are able to watch them surface in our mind as we label other people's actions as "wrong," "bad," or "foolish." Yet we seem much less inclined to examine ourselves. Perhaps we are living well, are always right, and cause very little trouble to others. That is one possibility. Or perhaps we are simply more skillful and open to judging others and less skillful in examining our own lives. If we do not develop the ability to reflect on and evaluate our own actions, then how can we be capable of offering a genuine apology?

We can easily be distracted by the question of right versus wrong. An incident occurs and we conclude that we have been wronged and are "owed" an apology. In the absence of such payment we harbor anger, resentment, and pain. Of course, others see things similarly. Consequently, a degree of mutual hostility and resentment is woven into the fabric of relationships.

Rightness and wrongness provide a blurry lens, at best. When I try honestly to look at certain situations, I am sometimes confused about what is right and what is wrong. If right and wrong could be so easily determined, then people would not disagree so often when judging the same situation. Naikan exchanges this blurry lens for a clear one, a lens that points only at ourselves: how have we caused trouble, harm, difficulty, or suffering to another? Even in situations where it is unclear about whether I am right or wrong, I have generally found it possible to see how I have caused the other person difficulty.

A friend of mine was expected at her mother's home for dinner one Sunday afternoon. She arrived forty-five minutes late. When she arrived her mother was very upset. Her mother said she was worried that something serious had happened, perhaps a car accident. My friend believed her mother's response was unreasonable. The "unreasonableness" of a person's response is a loophole we often use to defend our own actions and diminish the importance of another's response. How can we truly know if any person's response is reasonable? What we do know is that my friend was late and that her mother was very anxious and upset. In abandoning the question of "reasonableness" my friend was able to see things from her mother's perspective. Whereas her defensiveness had placed distance between her and her mother, her apology brought them closer together. Most importantly, she saw the reality of her life in this particular situation. Perhaps her tardiness was unavoidable. Perhaps it was not possible for her to even call and say she would be late. Apologizing does not always mean that we will change our behavior. That is another choice we have to make. But in seeing the reality of how we cause harm to others, we can make that choice based on a more accurate picture of reality.

Periodically, we may offer an apology that somehow seems insincere. When I was a child, my mother would tell me to say I was sorry. I said the words but they were empty; I had no real awareness of the impact of my actions on others. My apology is empty of awareness when I fail to truly reflect on how I have caused the other person trouble or difficulty. We sometimes offer such apologies to escape honest self-reflection. At other times these "mindless" apologies are only strategies that, when offered quickly, attempt to avoid conflict and preserve a false sense of harmony. Is it possible that the sincerity of our apology is not a function of whether we feel sorry but whether we have truly reflected on ourselves?

If we have reflected sincerely on our own behavior—tried to see our contribution to a disagreement or problem and put ourselves in another's shoes—then we have moved closer to an honest reconciliation with the person we have hurt. Our apology will often be a natural response to seeing how others have suffered or been inconvenienced by our words and acts. In some cases feelings of remorse, regret, and sorrow will arise naturally. But if they do not, we cannot create them through our willpower. Nor can we demand such feelings from others. Feeling remorse is more grace than effort.

Sometimes an apology does not go far enough. Sometimes it is possible and necessary to offer something more than words. We may find that we can do something to rectify a situation, make amends for the harm we have done. When I have transgressed, I am fortunate if I can find situations that allow me to make amends for the damage. Restitution, where possible, does not benefit only the injured party, but the transgressor as well.

In other cases, an apology or offer of restitution may simply cause additional suffering. So even when we apologize, we must consider the trouble our apology may cause. Perhaps this was true of my wedding apology. Sometimes self-reflection is as far as we should go, lest we reopen old wounds and run up our karmic bill.

In situations where I am the recipient of someone else's apology, it is important that I understand the effort, discomfort, and grace that must have accompanied his own introspection. To have someone reflect, even momentarily, on how he has troubled me is to have someone try to touch me with the deepest understanding of which he is capable. Rather than forgive him, it is better to reflect on my own conduct and ask for his forgiveness.

Beyond Forgiveness

One cannot walk two paths at the same time, particularly when they go in different directions. If we reflect on our past, most of us will find instances in which others have hurt or wronged us. We may become absorbed by these memories and thoughts. Indeed, we may be guided by others toward absorption with these events based on the assumption that this process is therapeutic. Our ultimate goal, we are told, is to forgive those who have caused us suffering and difficulty—parents, former business partners, ex-wives, old friends, or criminals. Once we are able to forgive, perhaps we will find release from our anger and resentment. Perhaps we will find inner peace and spiritual rest. Perhaps the demons of the past will finally be banished forever. Taking this path can require a great deal of time and energy. Sometimes it takes years of counseling, which costs a great deal of money. But is this path really "therapeutic," and is it a path with a heart?

When Freud developed the foundation of contemporary Western psychology one hundred years ago, he departed from another path: religion and spirituality. This departure was not necessarily all bad, but he left behind several elements that were essential to the well-being of the human mind and spirit. One of those elements was self-reflection, the willingness of a human being to honestly and sincerely examine his conduct and relationships. But forgiveness requires us to examine and judge the conduct of others. In Japanese, this critical examination of the conduct of others is

> **"We need lots of love to forgive, but we need much more humility to ask for forgiveness."**
> MOTHER TERESA

sometimes referred to as *gaikan*. *Gaikan* involves focusing on the faults, mistakes, and transgressions of others. We notice others. We judge them. We bring our attention to our own discomfort, pain, and inconvenience. And then, often with a certain moral superiority, we forgive them. But Naikan self-reflection serves to redirect us back to our own conduct and treatment of others, advice that can be found in the ancient Buddhist *Dhammapada:*

> *Look not at the faults of others,*
> *at what they have done or left undone;*
> *rather, look at what you yourself*
> *have done or left undone.*
> [verse 50]

I believe that the energy we devote to trying to forgive others (or even ourselves) is misdirected. The more we focus on the "sins" of others, the more we nourish resentment and anger in ourselves. But the true path of self-reflection can be a meaningful journey for many reasons. First, evaluation of our own conduct is more useful if our purpose is learning and self-improvement. Second, awareness of our own mistakes and selfishness brings us a healthy dose of humility, a valuable asset both spiritually and in human relations. Third, examination of our conduct toward others in light of the support we have received from them opens the door to spiritual/religious experience, providing a foundation for gratitude and faith in a power beyond ourselves. Finally, I believe in the profound capacity of openness and honesty to aid us in acknowledging who we are and what we've done. Our healing comes much more from accepting the reality of the things we have done to hurt others—

S(s)elf-Esteem

Arrogance is foolishness. Pride is unrealistic.
The discovery of humility is pain.
Humility, itself, is freedom.
Pride in one's humility is seductive and dangerous.
Self-esteem is an illusion when it is esteem for the self.
Esteem for the Self is Wisdom.
Guilt is natural. Compassion is natural.
Two ends of the same stick.
Gratitude is the natural response to opening one's eyes.
Moments of seeing—gifts themselves.
Clinging to unreality is demanding and exhausting.
Reality is just as it is.
Make your image a realistic one.
Disappear into the mystery of being ordinary.
It's a long fall, but the ground is soft and firm.

lying to our parents, cheating our former business partners, deceiving our former lovers—than from condemning others for what they have done to us. Ultimately we may find that we are in no position to grant forgiveness, and that we have received forgiveness before we even had the presence of mind to ask for it.

The Game of Forgiv-e-Ball

There is a distant land in which the people play a game similar to our American game of football. As you know, football can be a very rough game, and the players often get knocked down and bruised. Part of the game of Forgiv-e-Ball is that whenever a player is hurt or hit, or is the subject of some painful act, that player must express forgiveness to the one who perpetrated the act. This is a central part of the game, which, in this distant land, is seen as a spiritual practice.

In fact, over the years, less and less of the players' training focuses on the game skills and more stress is placed on the spiritual preparation for forgiveness. The training can be very intense, with players remembering all the ways they have been hurt in their personal lives and trying to reexperience their previous pain. They watch videotapes of plays where they were injured in games and practice reciting phrases of forgiveness toward the players who hurt them. Points are given to the team whose players are the most forgiving. There are awards at the end of each game for the "Most Forgiving Player" (MFP).

Because these spiritually advanced players attract large crowds, their salaries are often very high. Many of them receive widespread acclaim for their "forgiveness accomplishments," and they write books and endorse spiritual products. Last year, however, there was a new rookie player on one of the more popular teams. The coaches had high expectations of him. But when the season started, every time he would run into or injure a player, he would apologize with the words, "I'm sorry," or "excuse me," or "please forgive me." The referees called penalties on him; the coaches were dismayed. The fans began to boo him. The league officials met and agreed that he was ruining the game. Something had to be done. He was called into the president's office and fired. He apologized for causing such a controversy.

They forgave him.

Even the Best of Intentions

During a residential training program, Jane began to make coffee for our group during the morning break. She found that someone had already inserted a filter and included the proper amount of coffee. She filled the empty glass pot with water and poured it into the machine, but to her surprise the machine had already been filled with water, so water, and coffee, began to flow everywhere. It was a great mess.

Jane had tried to do something helpful for others and created a mess instead. What about the person who had prepared the coffeemaker before Jane arrived? That person had also tried to be of service by getting everything ready ahead of time so others would go to less trouble. But since Jane had no way of seeing that there was water in the coffeemaker, the end result was a mess and wasted water. So both individuals, though perhaps well motivated, seemed to have caused trouble for the other and for the rest of the group.

I also often have good intentions to be of service or assistance and yet end up causing trouble instead. It saddens me when I reflect on all the troubles I have caused others, even when my intentions were to be helpful. Once I washed my wife's clothes, only to find out later that I had shrunk her favorite blouse. On several occasions I have called my mother in an effort to be pleasant and loving and ended up in an argument with her. No matter how hard I try, I frequently cause trouble where I desire to be helpful.

There are times when reflection upon my trouble-causing nature brings frustration or despair. To have such a great yearning to be wise, kind, and loving and to have to confront the reality of my selfishness and foolishness can be painful. Yet even as I fail in my attempts to do good, life supports and cares for me—not because I've earned it or deserve it, but in spite of my mistakes and selfishness. When we see the reality of the troubles we have caused along with the support we have received, our attempts to fool others and to fool ourselves may melt away, leaving us to live a more natural and realistic life.

To live naturally is to just be a human being. There is a Zen poet named Ryokan who wrote a poem about a maple leaf:

Maple leaf
showing front
showing back
falling down

It is a simple but lovely poem with a wonderful lesson about life. When a maple leaf falls it just falls. It does not try to conceal one side of itself from the rest of the world. It does not try to "look good" to others. When Ryokan saw the maple leaf, he became aware of his continuing efforts to show only his best side. He bowed to the maple leaf out of admiration for its naturalness and openness.

When I try to live the life of a maple leaf, my efforts alone place me light-years away from such a life. Even the idea of such a life is filled with my ego-centered desires to look good to others. To try to be a maple leaf or to be proud of one's humility—what foolishness this is. As I write I cannot help but laugh at these aspects of my own nature. Such things cause me to cry in one moment and to laugh in another. Sometimes I cry and laugh without trying.

A group of Jane's colleagues come to Jane's assistance and clean up the watery mess. A new pot of coffee is made. It's not very long before Jane is sitting in a comfortable chair with a hot cup of coffee made just the way she likes it. Trying to help, she is helped. Trying to serve, she is served. Life isn't very trying. Only the trying is.

Mysteries and Myths of Separation

We have invested a lifetime of attention and energy in maintaining ourselves as separate and independent. We put up fences, lock our doors, and attend to our needs and goals with a certain confidence about the boundaries between us and not-us. But as we reflect on ourselves, the nature of those boundaries becomes questionable. We begin to see that our bodies, our stuff, even our ideas and words are musical arrangements whose notes come from somewhere else.

It is a bit shocking to have our basic identity questioned. It has impli-

> "A good case can be made for our nonexistence as entities. We are not made up, as we had always supposed, of successively enriched packets of our own parts. We are shared, rented, 'occupied.'"
>
> LEWIS THOMAS

cations that go far beyond what name appears on our business cards. What happens when we discover that we can't "win" an argument with a family member? What responsibilities arise when we become caretakers rather than owners of our "stuff?" How do we resolve the confusion that accompanies the awareness that the role of victim and that of perpetrator are not as black-and-white as we thought they were? What replaces the pride in our accomplishments when we become conscious of the web of people and things that made those accomplishments possible?

We have developed a certain comfort with the illusion of separateness. It may please me to think that my life, my decisions, and my body are my own. It is my defense against others telling me what I should do. It is my defense against having to accept some responsibility for the problems of our society or our planet. But there is no real security to be found in this illusion of separateness. No peace. And no truth.

If we are willing to investigate our connectedness, a whole new experience of life unfolds. We feel supported and cared for. We feel related to people we have never met. Our extended family extends everywhere. This path of connectedness can lead us to the doorstep of faith. It can lead us to the doorstep of our true purpose in life. It can inspire us, delight us, and free us from the burden of self-importance. But first we must let go of who we think we are.

Who Am I?

Have you thanked your mitochondria today? As we continue to investigate who we are, who is the "I" that is conducting the investigation? Discoveries in the last quarter century have shed light on our biological makeup and called into question our assumption that we are an identity separate from the rest of the world. At the interior of our cells are small entities called mitochondria. Mitochondria are like tiny power plants designed to convert oxygen and nutrients into usable energy for this body I have always thought belonged to "me." These creatures swim around in the cytoplasm of our body's cells. A single cell may contain from tens to hundreds of them. Functioning as a biological power plant, they produce the fuel for all the activities of the body's cells. Without the mitochondria, we could not move our toe, blink our eyelids, or even think a thought. As molecular biologist David Clayton explains, "The alternative to functioning mitochondria is called death."

What is particularly interesting is that these little entities are not really "ours." They maintain their own DNA, a kind of genetic map, which is quite different from "our" DNA, which is stored inside the cell's nucleus. The mitochondria maintain themselves and reproduce in their own fashion. These little entities resemble much more the germs that cause Rocky Mountain spotted fever or the bacteria on the roots of beans than they do "us." Yet they populate the human body in great numbers. Biologist Lewis Thomas estimates that "there is almost as much of them in sheer dry bulk as there is the rest of me."

The discovery of mitochondria and their unusual character casts biological doubt on the fundamental nature of our separate identity. We may readily admit that we exist in an interdependent state with the world "out there," needing food, water, and air for basic survival. But now it appears that we exist interdependently with entities "in here," requiring their efforts just to move our eyes across this page.

So what is really "out there" and "in here"? Where does "me" end and "not-me" begin? Where are the boundaries between "us" and "not-us"? Surely it is not this thin layer of skin that encloses this body. The body always appeared to be our clearly definable identity. Its perimeter was our national security boundary. Everything inside this three-dimensional line is my territory: Don't cross this line. Don't touch "me." But how do we explain our tears when we see a picture of a starving child in Africa? How do we explain the feeling of joy when we hear that a baby was just rescued from the rubble of an earthquake in India? These events "out there" sometimes touch us "in here." When we consider mitochondria, or childbirth, or composting, the question of our identity begins to blur. Perhaps our bodily boundaries are simply an illusion. We seem to be tenants who are simultaneously subletting our space and, from time to time, we ponder, and search for, the landlord.

We are not the only beings to be graced by the efforts of mitochondria. They exist in birds, dolphins, seaweed, my dog, and the little squirrels who cleverly invent ways to invade the bird feeder on my porch. Thomas writes of the mitochondria,

> Through them I am connected; I have close relatives, once removed, all over the place. This is a new kind of information, for me, and I regret somewhat that I cannot be in closer touch with my mitochondria. . . . I cannot help thinking that if only I knew more about them, and how they maintain our synchrony, I would have a new way to explain music to myself.

I must admit that throughout my entire life, or at least until recently, I have taken mitochondria for granted. I did not thank them, or appreciate them, or intentionally do anything for them. I just continued to live my life: eating, breathing, blinking, talking, thinking, and, every once in a while, pondering the question of who I am. All the while the mitochondria community was working round the clock to pump out enough energy so these things could be done. They've done a pretty good job, I think.

So as I look at what I'm writing, I say thank you to the mitochondria in my optic nerve. And while I'm at it, I might as well thank the rest of them for all their hard work over these many years. But the energy for saying thank you or for writing it, or even thinking it, comes from the efforts of the mitochondria. Without them, thank-yous would be impossible. So I can't even say thank you without help. But then, who is it that's really doing the thanking?

The Roots of Stuff

I am surrounded by stuff—some of it useful, some of it charming, some of it wobbly. Every once in a while I enjoy taking an inventory of this stuff to see where it came from. As I trace its roots I become more aware of the intricate web of people and materials that supports my life in a material way.

I am sitting in the living room of my home, although I actually rent, rather than own, this house since my family resides at the education and retreat center where I am the director. Some of the "stuff" in this room is also owned by the center. The comfortable green sofa I'm sitting on, for example. And the woodstove that warms the room. And the dining room hanging fixture. I treat these things as my own, even though they're not. They're someone else's. I get to use them.

In the corner is a black upright piano. Inside that piano is an older, smaller brown piano. The brown piano is the one purchased by my parents so that I could take piano lessons when I was ten years old. After college I moved to Virginia and my parents let me take the piano with me. A few years later I decided to buy a new piano, so I sold the little brown piano and used the money as a down payment on a lovely new one. At the time, I didn't even consider returning the money to my mom and dad. I don't think I even told them I was selling their piano, which apparently I had confiscated on the basis of its occupation of space in my house. Periodically, when I sit down to play, my piano reminds me of its ancestor, without whom it wouldn't be here right now.

On top of the piano is a delightful wood sculpture of a coyote given to us by Kris, someone who did Naikan at the center many years ago. It appears as if the coyote is howling, trying to drown out my piano playing out of consideration of others who might be in the room. The sculpture is made of beautiful wood, perhaps cherry, which came from a tree of course. And on its way to the top of my piano it was sawed, transported, carved, stained, and displayed by a small army of folks

> **"We ourselves are not masters of our own ability and knowledge. They, like our talents and health, are a loan presented for our use. We must live as people who know that such temporary possessions are not true belongings and that we must give account for our management of them."**
> ALBERT SCHWEITZER

who used tools, machines, and other objects developed by a larger army of folks.

There's an oak table in the dining room, the history of which I know very little since my sole claim to its ownership is that I married its owner. It's a lovely round table with a few wobbly chairs, and it has served me (and I've served others on it) for more than ten years.

On the floor near the piano is a stack of meditation cushions (*zafu*), two of which were made by Mrs. Tsuji, the wife of a Buddhist priest who was a teacher of mine for many years. The stitching on the cushions has been reliable enough to withstand my weight for nearly twenty years. Hanging on the wall near the cushions is an arrangement of small dried flowers, elegantly pressed under glass and framed by oak. It was given to us by Sue, a longtime friend and former president of our board of directors. The roots of this wall decoration include the actual roots of those flowers, and the sun and rain and soil that allowed them to grow. I don't know the person who actually assembled this lovely piece of art, but her work has been a delight to my eye on many occasions.

From the living room I can see a copper-bottomed pot sitting on the kitchen stove—a gift, perhaps ten years ago, from Julie. I couldn't even begin to count how many soups my wife and I have cooked in that pot. And I know nothing about the process of mining copper, but I'm guessing it takes more than a few people and machines to transform it from a mineral embedded in the earth to the bottom of a pot.

I use the stuff and am served by it nearly every day of my life. Some of it provides utility and some of it provides beauty. I like being aware of the generation that passed it on to me, but even more I like to reflect on the invisible people who created it and the materials that were reshaped and the tools that were needed and the people who originally invented those tools and . . . before very long I am absorbed in a very different vision of my stuff and my life. These things are no longer "mine." Rather, I am a caretaker of this unusual collection of objects that have decided to share this house with me for a brief period of time. I will outlive some of this stuff, which will break, and die, and be relocated to a landfill somewhere to make room for replacements. But some of this stuff will outlive me as my own body stops working and finds its own "landfill," and, just like my piano, I will be replaced by something with a more youthful tone and fewer blemishes on the finish.

Perhaps the most basic conclusion I can draw from reflecting on all this stuff is that it's all made from other stuff. You can examine any item, including yourself, and you will find that it is simply a collection and arrangement of other items. Inevitably, whether we're a human being or a sofa, we must pass on the credit for our existence to our ingredients and the cooks who mixed us up and baked us. It's easy to forget where our stuff came from. And when we forget, we simply label it all as "mine" and see ourselves as the master of our isolated, independent material world. But when we pause and reflect on the roots of all this stuff, we get connected, in both time and space, to the web of interdependence that surrounds us and is us. In such a world, how can we feel unloved? And how can we ever be lonely?

My Heart Is Your Heart

My wife and I were cross-country skiing at a place called Blueberry Hill, in the Green Mountains. It had just started to snow and the fresh flakes made a soft cushion for us as we glided up and down through the white hills. I had just finished a rather steep climb and was pausing to catch my breath. But it couldn't be caught, as each breath simply disappeared—first into my lungs, and then into the sky. I noticed the intense pounding of my heart, which created a vibration all the way across my chest. My heart made the noticing possible. Underneath several layers of clothes I could feel the moisture against my skin. A massive exchange was going on at this very moment. Moisture, heat, and air were going from "in here" to "out there." And the air out there, with its life-giving oxygen and invisible little creatures, was being sucked "in here" and feeding my blood, brain, heart, and other organs. A snowflake landed on my lip and I tasted its wet coldness. The images of snow clumps resting on the evergreens and yellow birches became my mind.

I know my skin is not the boundary between me and out there. Yet it's easy to forget this and mistake this body and its contents as "mine," something with a clear identity that I own. And since I own it, I can do what I like with it, right? I can poison it with smoke, inflate it with fat, saturate it with alcohol. It's my body and I'll do as I please, thank you.

> "My heart is your heart, your heart is my heart; to become mine . . . is your heart."
>
> SAICHI

But reality has ways of reminding us who we are and who we aren't. For when this body breathes out, the rest of the world breathes in.

Science has a way of pointing this out. It can identify tobacco toxins in the lungs of children who don't smoke. It shows us how viruses and bacteria are transferred from one person to another. It demonstrates how chemicals in spray cans and factory chimneys affect the atmosphere and weather. Science often allows human beings to see what can't normally be seen. And we're sternly reminded of who we are. We love this knowledge in church, in prayer, and in meditation. It's refreshing and renewing to be reminded that we are more than just a little collection of working parts that will someday stop working. But when it comes to our health, many of us resent this same wisdom. Just a little. We don't want to be told that what we do impacts on others. We're a bit uncomfortable with responsibility for *everyone's* health, for *everything's* health. So we tighten our fingers around our ignorance and close our eyes. This preserves, momentarily, our illusion of independence in a world that is interdependent.

We don't have to be scientists to recognize the impact of our health on others. It's revealed in health insurance rates and taxes. It's revealed in the efforts of our family to care for us when we are sick and can no longer care for ourselves. Most tragically, it's revealed in the tears of a child whose mother or father has died from a fully preventable disease. It saddens me, because when I stand next to that child at the funeral, I'm breathing in when she is breathing out. I'm drinking her tears in my glass of water. And the grief in her heart, in some inexplicable way, seems to bring sadness into my own heart. What greater proof do we need that the ripples of health, as well as sickness, reverberate throughout the universe?

So when you exercise today, or do yoga, or eat a healthful meal, it's not just your body you're caring for. And when you see someone jogging or riding a bicycle, it's not just their health that's at stake.

My wife is skiing just ahead of me. I watch her body weight shift from side to side as she glides down the trail. She leaves tracks in her wake that make it easier for me to follow. Thank you, Linda. I'm lucky to be married to a woman who takes such good care of her body. Our body. Eventually, her body, my body, all our bodies will stop working. We'll be gone, just as all this snow will melt in spring. But while we're here there's lots to do. We have this amazing opportunity to do something useful, something meaningful, with our lives. And we're given a body to make this possible. How perfect! How purposeful! What shall we do with such an extraordinary gift?

Illness and Faith

One of the best times to practice Naikan reflection is when you are struggling with an illness or disease. This is often a time when we become very self-centered and we have the attitude, "Why did this happen to me?" We can become so wrapped up in our pain and discomfort that we lose sight of the care and support we are receiving from the world, even as we struggle with our illness. Rev. Shundo Aoyama, a Buddhist priest, states,

> If we have to be ill, let us meet it head on. Let us welcome our illness with open arms. Let us live in such a way that we are grateful that our illness helps us improve our character. We should use

the time of our illness to think about aspects of life that escaped us when we were healthy.

To "welcome our illness with open arms" is one of life's greatest challenges. Periodically I work with those who have cancer, AIDS, and other severe illnesses. I ask these individuals to reflect on the period of time just after they received some major treatment such as surgery or chemotherapy. During the following week, what did you receive from others? Did someone cook or serve your meals? Did others visit you or call you while you were hospitalized? Did you receive books, magazines, or other gifts? Who washed your clothes? Who paid your medical bills? Did you have use of a telephone, a television, and electric lights? How many people gave time and effort so these conveniences could be made available to you? What did your spouse or partner do for you? What did the doctors and nurses do for you? While you were suffering and in pain, what else was going on? If we only notice and remember our suffering, we create additional suffering, unrealistic and unnecessary suffering.

Throughout most of my adult life, I have been fortunate to have very good health, but we should be careful not to take credit for our good health, for ultimately we cannot escape sickness and death, and our good health is as much a consequence of grace than any of our own efforts. I learned this a few years ago when I contracted some type of illness, probably a virus, that made me extremely sick for two weeks. Even though it was not a life-threatening disease, I had not been so ill for fifteen years. For many days I had a fever and I would have hot flashes and break out in a sweat day and night. For three successive nights I could not sleep for more than an hour at a time, and my entire body was aching and sore. I had a hard cough,

Pine Needles

Withered, brown pine needles
dangling from a web of lush, green branches.
They shall be washed away
by the same spring rain
which gives life
to the sleeping buds.

HO SEN

and whenever I would cough it would send shooting pains up into my skull. During the second week, my entire head was filled with congestion and I had difficulty breathing. My head felt like a solid block of ice and I had constant head pain. Even while in bed or on a sofa, it was difficult to find any respite from this discomfort.

Compared to people with truly serious diseases, these symptoms amount to little more than discomfort and inconvenience. Yet I was humbled by how challenging even a small illness can be. I think I have much greater compassion now for people who are struggling with chronic illness.

During the days of my illness I would try to maintain the presence of mind to do Naikan reflection, even for a few minutes. After I had almost fully recovered, I went into the forest and quietly reflected at length on the previous two-week period. Following is a limited version of my Naikan reflection on my life during that time.

What Did I Receive during My Period of Illness?

I received a comfortable bed for rest and sleep with a warm down blanket and soft pillows. My wife provided a fresh change of linens several times during this period. I received hot water, a shower, and fresh towels, and three times my wife gave me a hot bath using eucalyptus oil, which helped me to breathe and relieved my cough and head pain temporarily. She suggested inhaling mint or eucalyptus added to boiling water, and this treatment also gave me periodic relief from congestion and coughing throughout the two weeks. Our stove and electricity made it possible to boil the water and create steam. I received about seventy-five tablets of vitamin C, supplied by the local natural foods store and my friend Hal, and my wife brought these home for me. I received herbs such as echinacea, goldenseal, licorice, and cayenne, supplied by a local herb shop and coming from a variety of medicinal plants. I received lozenges that helped soothe my throat. I had unlimited use of water from our well, and a hot pot allowed me to make herb teas quickly and easily. My wife made a poultice to warm my chest one night, and our landlady's sofa provided a comfortable resting place where I could keep my head propped up. I received the use of over five hundred tissues for my nose and some aloe lotion, which helped to heal the irritation around my nose. My wife has much knowledge of natural healing and many books, and I received the benefit of her informed advice. She would often make me fresh juices in the morning before she left for work, and on one occasion she returned home at lunchtime to check on me and fix a healthy meal for me. I received heat from the furnace and oil, and the walls and roof of the house protected me from wind, cold, snow, and rain. I received the use of a telephone and telephone lines, which allowed me to maintain contact with the outside world from the comfort of my home. A radio made it possible to listen to news, and my wife periodically brought home newspapers for me to read. I had many good books available to me, including two gift books from Jim Roberts and Perri Ardman. My dog provided me with constant companionship and gave me a good excuse to take a walk and get some fresh air on days when that was possible. The flexibility of my job allowed me to work and rest as needed. Even though I worked far less than normal during this time, I still received my full salary. My wife took on most of the household errands and chores, including bringing home the mail, preparing meals, washing the dishes, and feeding the dog and taking him for a morning walk. She provided me with wonderful nursing care, which included a rented movie one evening, a homemade carrot cake, and an ongoing stock of fresh fruits, vegetables, and salad greens to help nourish me as I began eating again. I received the use of a toilet to discharge what my body could not use. I received a get-well card from my mother-in-law, and

> "The headache also taught me about Naikan. We have a tendency to remember the times when people behaved in ways we did not like. 'He never told me he loved me,' or 'She didn't pay enough attention to me.' We pay more attention to the 'bad' things and use them as excuses. Noticing my tendency to be aware of the pain in my head at the expense of all the other, much lighter and often pleasant sensations in other areas of my body, I realized how much reality I shut out, as if it didn't exist."
>
> KATANNYA VAN TYLER

the service of my body's immune system, which works in ways that are a mystery to me.

What Did I Give during My Period of Illness?

I can think of very little I gave to others during my illness. I walked the dog about six or seven times. I fed the birds almost every day and washed some of my wife's clothing on one or two occasions. One morning, when I was feeling better, I made my wife breakfast. I sewed up a hole in a sock and did some work in the garden, turning the compost and preparing the soil. I set up an indoor lighting system for the garden seedlings. That's about all I can remember.

What Troubles and Difficulties Did I Cause Others?

I canceled a canoe trip with my friend Ken and rescheduled a telephone meeting with my board president, giving her only two hours notice. I fell behind on all aspects of my work, from tax payments to writing and editing, and this will inconvenience many people to greater and lesser degrees. I generally left the kitchen area messy each day with empty teacups and plates, which my wife would then wash after coming home from a full day's work. My illness burdened her more than anyone else. On nights when I couldn't sleep, I would toss and turn and get in and out of bed, disturbing her own sleep. She had the added burden of doing many of the household errands and often had to listen to my complaints about my pain, discomfort, and tiredness. When I would go to bed early, I would forget to set the alarm and she would have to set it later, trying to do so without disturbing me. I caused my wife frustration by not always following her advice, and on one occasion I expressed anger at her openly, even though she had been caring for me for more than a week. I was a very unattractive person to look at during this time, and I did a poor job of trying to keep up a neat appearance, showing very little concern for others who had to look at me. I also caused trouble to my clothing by throwing it on the chair by the bed, rather than folding it or hanging it in the closet.

* * *

These were the conditions of my life during my illness, and in reflecting on this period I have become intimately aware of the care and support that was given to me. Similarly, I am aware of my own weaknesses and how I have been a source of difficulty and inconvenience to others. Such awareness brings us to the doorstep of religious faith. When we give up on ourselves, when we feel hopeless and powerless, then our heart is opened to the true compassion and love of a Power Beyond Ourselves. While I was ill, I considered the story of a famous Buddhist priest of the nineteenth century named Manshi Kiyozawa. As the story relates, at one point everything was going well for him. He held an important teaching position in the Otani-ha sect of Pure Land Buddhism. He married into a family of some status. He was young and healthy. His worldly life was marked by success. But then, suddenly, everything changed. He lost his job and was even excommunicated from the sect because of political changes in the Buddhist hierarchy. Then he contracted tuberculosis. He found himself sick and unemployed and living off the goodwill of his father-in-law. Yet it was during this time that he claims to have experienced true religious faith. He kept a diary, entitled *December Fan,* so named because he felt as useless as a Japanese fan in the middle of winter. In his diary, only a few years before his death, he wrote,

> What is the most important thing to do in the effort to improve ourselves? First, reflect upon yourself. By seeing the reality of yourself, you will gain insight into the path of heaven.

Kiyozawa was able to realize the futility of his own self-efforts. As a result, he attained freedom, by completely entrusting his life to a Power Beyond Self. Illness can be the door to such freedom, if we are willing to reflect on ourselves and our life in a sincere and honest way.

Intimate Attention

It was Steve and Cindy's first meeting with me. Cindy was in another room doing Naikan reflection while I met with Steve. Steve explained:

> "Love is not a matter of getting what you want. Quite the contrary. The insistence on always having what you want, on always being satisfied, on always being fulfilled, makes love impossible."
> THOMAS MERTON

"We share an interest in music and we both play piano. I would really like us to play duets together. It means a lot to me. But Cindy won't honor this request. Sight-reading music is more difficult for her and she won't make the effort to practice. It's really important to me that we play together. I'm very hurt and angry that she won't do this."

"Is there something that is similarly important to her?"

There is a long pause. "I don't know. Probably. I've never asked."

Where is Steve's attention? It's not unusual for us to focus on what the other person can do to make us happy. But is that really what a loving relationship is about? How often have we thought of our partner and said, "If he/she really loved me . . ."? What is the alternative, one that involves a shift of attention to "If I really loved him/her . . ."? To shift from the former to the latter is to shift our attention from our own self-centered needs to the needs of our partner.

Most of us have never been trained to shift our attention like this. In fact, contemporary Western psychotherapy has generally promoted values that discourage us from service and self-sacrifice. The contemporary emphasis is on "getting my needs met" and "taking care of number one."

I can think of no worse formulae for a relationship. Each of the partners asserting their needs and demands, primarily concerned about their own happiness, and unwilling to examine themselves as a source of conflict and difficulty—can two people love each other and find meaning in such a relationship?

At best, this type of relationship establishes a contract as a replacement for love. The contract states, "If

> "Once the realization is accepted that even between the closest human beings infinite distances continue, a wonderful living side by side can grow, if they succeed in loving the distance between them which makes it possible for each to see the other whole against the sky."
> RAINER MARIA RILKE

you continue to do these things and make me happy, I will continue to remain in the relationship with you and also do certain things." This may be a sound basis for having our house painted or buying heating oil, but most relationships will eventually collapse under this arrangement. Sooner or later one partner fails to hold up his or her end of the bargain. Unless there is a firmer foundation than a "contract" and a greater purpose than "my happiness," it may be the beginning of the end. Indeed, more than half of all marriages will end in divorce. We walk away resentful, complaining, and having great insights into the transgressions and faults of our former partner.

While we thus reassure ourselves, the source of our suffering remains unchanged.

Gaikan: The Misdirection of Attention

Whereas Naikan means "inside observation," the word *gaikan* means "outside observation." I use it to describe the misdirection of attention toward judging and changing others. When we're noticing our parents, spouse, or business associates and judging and criticizing their conduct, we're doing *gaikan*. When our focus is on how the other person needs to change, to improve the way he or she is living, we're doing *gaikan*. When we're blaming others, attending to their weaknesses, faults, and limitations, we're doing *gaikan*. If we spend a great deal of time doing *gaikan,* we will become good at it.

> **"If you judge people, you have no time to love them."**
> MOTHER TERESA

The great thirteenth-century Sufi poet Rumi appropriately illustrates *gaikan* in one of his teaching stories. He tells of four Indians who enter a mosque, kneel to the floor, and begin deep, sincere praying. When the priest walks by them, one of the Indians looks up and, without thinking, begins to speak:

> "Oh, are you going to give the call to prayers now? Is it time?"
> The second Indian turns and whispers, "You spoke. Now your prayers are invalid."
> The third said, "Uncle, don't scold him! You've done the same thing. Correct yourself."
> The fourth, also out loud, said, "Praise to God, I haven't made the mistake of these three."
> So all four prayers are interrupted, with the three fault-finders more at fault than the original speaker! Blessed is one who sees his weakness, and blessed is one who, when he sees a flaw in someone else, takes responsibility for it.

There are several dilemmas one encounters in doing *gaikan*. First, we cannot control the actions of others. We may notice the faults of others and prescribe changes, but often these prescriptions are not filled. We suggest that this person needs to stop smoking, that person needs to lose weight, another person needs to drive more carefully.

If we examine our experience, isn't it true that much of the time people don't do what we tell them?

So we are left with feelings of frustration because our desires for others, even desires that spring from genuine concern, are not fulfilled. We are left with feelings of powerlessness, because, in reality, we cannot control the behavior of others. Disappointment, resentment, hopelessness—all arise from our efforts to "work on" the lives of others rather than ourselves.

And what is our response to this predicament? Often we continue to judge and try to change others, but with more force and determination. We act from an assumption that, if only we put more energy, repetition, and strength into our efforts to change others, they will bend to our will. But the more we push the more they resist. We damage our relationships and, most importantly, we distract ourselves from our own self-reflection and attention to what we are doing.

Al-Anon, an organization for family members of alcoholics, is also concerned about misdirected attention. They clearly advise participants that the drinking or nondrinking of others cannot be controlled or managed. What can be controlled is our own conduct. If the alcoholic stops drinking,

> this is indeed a miracle, but it is not our miracle; it is the alcoholic's. It is not our business (nor has it ever been!) to watch over him, worry about his sobriety, see that he doesn't drink, that he goes to the right number of AA meetings. If we continue the techniques of management and supervision that did so much to make a mess of life during drinking days, we're headed for trouble.

Even if we could change others, how could we know what is best for another person? In reflecting on my own life, I see a multitude of mistakes that serve as trail markers for my memory. Many times I made poor choices. Often I caused difficulty for others and trouble for myself. Since I have such a mediocre track record of my own, I can only conclude that I am in no position to judge, with any competence, what another person needs to do. No matter how clear-cut another person's situation may appear to me, I cannot know the actual experience of his life. If I am honest, I must always admit that my judgment may be, and has been, wrong.

Seeing Yourself through the Eyes of Your Partner

What would it be like to be your partner who has to deal with you on a daily basis? What does she (or he) see when she first looks at you each morning? What household habits does she find most annoying? How do you think she feels when you read the newspaper while you are having breakfast and she is talking to you? How much time has she spent waiting for you because you were late during the past month? How many times has she been criticized by you? How many hours has she listened to you complain about your work or your family or your health? How close can you come to putting yourself in her shoes, to understanding her frustration and fear, to seeing yourself through her eyes?

Mostly, we see things only from our own self-centered perspective. If it rains and I am supposed to play golf, I get angry, but the farmer down the road is pleased because his crops need water. If I can briefly step outside myself, I may get a glimpse of life from another perspective. I may get a glimpse of myself from another perspective. Naikan reflection provides an opportunity for me to know my partner and to know myself more intimately and realistically.

AN EXAMPLE OF NAIKAN

A Man Reflects on Himself in Relation to His Wife

What I Received from Her

1. She came to Los Angeles with me to visit my parents.
2. For my birthday I received a book, a travel umbrella, and a lovely pasta dinner.
3. She picked me up at the train station when I returned from a business trip.
4. On the return trip from L.A. she drove more than half the time when I was feeling tired.
5. She helped me wash and wax my car.
6. She exercises and eats healthful food, thereby continuing to be an attractive, strong, and healthy partner.
7. She washed, dried, and put away my clothes at least twenty times.
8. I received her sexual affection and attention on at least twenty-five occasions.
9. She took responsibility for contraception whenever we made love to each other.
10. She handled the financial responsibilities of paying the bills and balancing the checkbook.
11. One evening when we were trying to decide which movie to see, she agreed to see the movie she knew I preferred.
12. She wrote a nice letter to my father.
13. She took telephone messages for me when I was away on business.
14. She ironed my shirt for me when I was late for work.
15. She took care of sending a wedding present to friends of

ours who live overseas.

16. She makes the bed nearly every morning.

17. She cleaned the house thoroughly when I had a business associate coming by.

18. She took the cat to the animal hospital for the cat's shots.

19. She gave me an aspirin when I had a headache and rubbed my shoulders.

20. She helped me pack for my business trip and hung my coat up and put away my clothes when I returned.

What I Gave to Her

1. I gave her a new raincoat and a stopwatch for keeping track of her running time.

2. I gave her a rose when she picked me up at the train station.

3. I gave her some cookies when I returned from the trip.

4. I visited a friend of hers in the hospital.

5. I made copies of some photos she liked.

6. I washed her clothes four times and took some dresses to the cleaners for her.

7. I mailed some important documents for her.

8. I gave her two back massages.

The Troubles and Difficulties I Caused Her

1. I incorrectly washed one of her blouses and the color faded.

2. I expressed frustration at her when I got lost while we were driving.

3. Because she went to L.A. with me, she had to work late several nights to finish a project before our trip.

4. I argued with her about the merits of a book she read, which was frustrating for her.

5. I caused her to be late for work one morning.

6. I caused her trouble by giving her cookies when she's trying to eat only healthful food.

7. I criticized her several times about how she handled a situation at work.

8. I woke her up when I called her late at night during my business trip.

9. I interrupted her at work six times by calling her.

10. I acted angry toward her when she arrived late for dinner, and I claimed that the dinner was ruined, even though it wasn't.

11. My train was late, causing her to wait an extra twenty-five minutes for me.

12. I flirted with a woman at a conference, which would have upset her if she knew. I deceived her by not mentioning it to her.

13. I ate the last piece of leftover lasagna one night when she had set it aside for her lunch for the following day.

14. I bought the wrong ingredient for a holiday dinner she was preparing and she had to make an extra trip to the store to get the correct one.

15. I took the library card from her purse to check out a book and didn't return it. When she went to the library and discovered that her card was missing, she thought she had lost it.

I received the following letter shortly after conducting a Naikan workshop that was given as part of a company's professional/personnel development program for its employees:

This is a note of thanks, not just from me but also from my wife. She does not know that she is thanking you yet, but she will in just a few days. We have been married (happily, I might add) for almost eighteen years now, and the biggest arguments that we get into are a misunderstanding of her worth and appreciation.

As a mother of five and a "stay-at-home-mom," she took care of most of the daily "chores" that are necessary. For that I never, or very seldom, thanked her. At least out loud. I always felt that those things were "her job" and I had mine. After all, she never thanked me for bringing home the paycheck. What I did not realize until today was that I got thanks at work, and she never did.

Starting today, I will be keeping a "running list" of the things that she does for me, and when the list gets more than one page, it will be delivered to her. I am guessing that she will be receiving one of these about every other day.

Thank you for your assistance in making this clear to me. I always thought about all that she did, I just never told her. See I have already started. I would never have written this type of note before.

Michael Reese

P.S. After going back only thirty-six hours, I have already filled my first page.

Attention to What's Not There

I always feel elated when I see the first hummingbirds in May. They zip to and fro, rediscovering the humming-bird feeder, which sometimes sways in the wind as it hangs from the awning. I enjoy seeing the red and yellow tulips squeeze up through the soil just out-

> "Poets have no right to picture love as blind; its blindfold must be removed so that it can have the use of its eyes."
> **BLAISE PASCAL**

side my office window. The goldfinch attempts to camouflage itself in the forsythia blossoms. It's hiding but it's there. Out in the garden I check the new seedlings of spinach and endive. They're small but healthy. But there's an empty patch in the garden where the buttercrunch lettuce is supposed to be. What happened? How come there's no lettuce coming up? My smile is suddenly stifled and my "mind of satisfaction" has become a "mind of disappointment." My attention has turned from what is there to what isn't there. There are other things that aren't there. The wildflowers haven't sprouted yet, neither have the lupins. The maple trees no longer are giving sap; not since mid-April. No more fresh maple syrup until next year. I haven't seen any deer for weeks. Nor have I seen the little ruffed grouse who used to follow me around the yard in winter.

It's extraordinary how something that's not there can block our view of what actually is there. While my mind was on "no deer," perhaps I missed another hummingbird. While my attention lingered on "no lettuce," perhaps I missed the scent of the lilac bush. And as my attention drifts to what I'm not getting from my partner, I become trapped in a cloud of what's not there. And the cloud gets thicker. And thicker. Until all I can see is what can't be seen.

A Fable: Giving, Receiving, and Desire-Ring

Once, a long time ago, a man and a woman fell deeply in love. They treated each other with such kindness and compassion that their love grew deeper each day. The man decided that he would give the woman a special gift on the eve of each full moon. So when the first full moon was ready to appear, he gave her a lovely wool scarf to keep her warm on even the coldest winter night. She was very touched and very grateful and once again they grew closer.

Now the man had a very unusual ring that he wore on the index finger of his right hand. Its stone had been cut from a ruby and gave off a glow that was quite entrancing. The woman had noticed this ring when they first met and had always admired it.

On the eve of the next full moon the man gave the woman an antique mirror so that she would see how beautiful she was. He always thought it was sad that she was unable to see herself the way he saw her. Again she was pleased and this time she returned his offering with a gift of her own, an antique pen with which he could write poetry and letters. He was pleased also and their love grew still deeper.

As time passed and they

"We did Naikan reflection on each year of our marriage. The first time I did this I told my teacher that I didn't cause Steven any trouble. On the contrary, he caused me trouble. I could remember very clearly how he hurt me. I had been carrying this hurt and anger throughout most of my marriage. Needless to say, the teacher had a very hard time believing I never hurt Steven and asked that I try again. I did try again and was troubled with what I wrote. There it was, staring me right in the face—all the ways I hurt Steven. I wasn't innocent. In fact, I was the cause of many of our troubles and difficulties. This was the hardest thing to admit and face. We have applied these approaches to our relationship since July of 1990 and I already exchanged gifts, she began to pay more and more attention to his ring, wondering if he would someday offer it to her as a gift. From time to time he considered giving away the ring. But each time he hesitated. The ring had such great value. Could he really give it away to somebody else? What if he gave her the ring and later found out that he had misplaced his trust in her or simply misjudged her? So he went out and bought her a different ring. It was a beautiful ring made of gold and silver. Still it could not compare with the ruby ring that he wore. No ring could.

When she saw the ring box she was very excited. But when she opened it and saw that it was not what she expected, she was disappointed. Why would he give her this ring instead? Perhaps he did not really love her. Perhaps he did not care about her at all. During the days that followed she found herself getting angry at him. He must have known what she wanted. Why was he being so cruel to her? And so for the first time a tension grew between them and the strength of their love was tested.

The next month he gave her a lovely gift again, but this time she was visibly angry with him and accused him of not really loving her. She confronted him with his failure to give her the ruby ring. But his own doubts about giving

> see the drastic change it has made in our marriage and in our life. Steven and I are more compassionate, accepting, loving, and overall, much happier. This is not to say that we don't fight. But our arguments are not as intense as before. We try to remember not to hurt one another. . . . I have to say it has been the best thing we could have done for our marriage."
>
> SHARON STEVENS

away the ring had been fueled by these recent events and now, more than before, he hesitated to part with it. The kindness and compassion with which they had once treated each other was gone. It was replaced by mistrust and anger.

In the following months he tried to make up for his selfishness by giving her the most wonderful gifts he could find. But it reached a point where every gift she received simply reminded her of what she wanted but was not getting, and so they were little appreciated and sometimes discarded with the trash. And then one day it seemed the love between them had completely vanished. All that remained was anger, mistrust, and disappointment. As they looked at one another they no longer saw the person they had fallen in love with.

There are lessons in this story about both giving and receiving.

Perhaps you'd care to complete the story. What is the likely ending? Can you discover an ending that will keep them together. How would you restimulate their feelings of love for one another? Or is it too late? If this couple came to you for counseling, what advice would you give to her? To him?

Relationships as a Vehicle for Training

Henry David Thoreau knew how to live alone. Really alone. A few of us may set up solitary housekeeping in a parcel of unexplored wilderness, but the vast majority will choose, and be

> "So a relationship is a great gift, not because it makes us happy—it often doesn't—but because any intimate relationship, if we view it as practice, is the clearest mirror we can find."
>
> **CHARLOTTE JOKO BECK**

chosen by, intimate partners. Such choices may be temporary, or . . . well, actually, temporary is your only option. These relationships are the graduate school of self-development. They provide us with the sharpest tools, the heaviest weights, and the thickest texts. They push us to our edge, stretch us beyond our limits. They may swing us on a pendulum from ecstasy and joy to the farthest reaches of pain and grief.

Here's an introductory catalogue of the program. Study it carefully. Know what you're getting into before you enroll.

Tuition: Just pay attention.

Registration: If you have an intimate partner you are already enrolled.

Faculty: The reality of what transpires between you and the other person—sex, romance, adultery, family problems, arguments, vacations, holidays, religious beliefs, and more.

Graduation: New courses are always being offered and you never seem to have enough credits.

Required text: Write your own.

COURSES

Attention 101

This is the basic course. If you flunk you have to take it again. If you pass, you have to take a refresher course right away. Quizzes and exams are frequent and unannounced. The question is always the same: Where is your attention? In this course you'll learn to shift your attention away from your needs and in the direction of your

Please Remind Me

by Gregg Krech

Please remind me of why I am here
when I am somewhere else.

When anger stirs
over unwashed dishes,
unkept promises,
and unpaid bills,

please soften my heart
and remind me
of why I am here.

When frustration is triggered
by the same argument
for the hundredth time,

please tame my words,
deepen my breath,
and remind me of why I am here.

When my attention is drawn
like a magnet
to myself—
my needs,
my wants,
my comfort,
my pain—

please blink my mind
and allow my eyes to see
into the heart of another,
that I may attend to their needs

and bear their pain
and be dissolved
into the reason I am here.

I know that reason
yet, so often,
I find myself somewhere else
and forget.
So please remind me.

Dedicated to Mary Claire Dehaven and Jim Scheid on their wedding day.

partner's needs. You'll learn to notice all that you receive from your partner, particularly "little" things (hint: there are no little things). You'll learn to say thank you as a response to receiving something. You'll learn the relationship between attention and being a caring, loving partner. As your attention widens, you qualify for the final exam: comparing everything you have received from your partner to what you have given. You grade your own exam. This course is a prerequisite to every other course. Without it, there is little you can learn elsewhere.

Homework: notice what you haven't noticed.

Humility and Transgressions 300

This is one of the toughest courses you'll take. You'll specifically look at how you have caused your partner trouble, difficulty, and inconvenience. You'll remember incidents in which you were selfish, argumentative, unreasonable, deceptive, and uncaring. You'll reflect on times when you attacked your partner with words. You'll consider all the times you've lied, or at least failed to tell the truth (quiz: is there really a difference?). You'll tell all these things to another human being (they've already taken this course). You'll confront fear, sadness, and guilt—lots of guilt, good, healthy guilt. Your ego and self-image are wounded. The former survives, the latter is changed, at least temporarily. In this course you'll learn a little about humility and reality and the connection between the two. You'll consider the real consequences of your behavior on your partner and identify ways you might make amends for the problems you have caused in the past. You pass the course when you are sincerely confused as to why the other person is still with you after all the troubles and suffering you have caused.

Homework: apology letters.

Gratitude 200

You'll learn about different ways to say thank you. You'll write thank-you letters and give thank-you gifts. You'll attempt to take nothing for granted (and fail repeatedly). You'll practice expressing appreciation for all that you are receiving. You'll make gifts for your partner. You'll do laboratory research where you'll experiment with giving affection and sexual attention without reciprocity, just giving (quiz: see if you can just give without taking anything). You'll learn to express thanks even when you don't feel grateful. You'll make several field trips to greeting card stores. This is a pleasant, fun course. Take it over and over again as many times as you like.

Homework: thank-you letters.

Job Descriptions 201

This course will help you define the boundaries of your education. It's really quite simple: your job is to work on yourself. It's not to change the other person. That's his job. You'll have an opportunity to not criticize or complain about the other person. The course appears simple but quickly becomes challenging as reality challenges you with behaviors of your partner that you would like to see change, such as smoking, eating poorly, not exercising, mistreatment of your family members, spending money, flirting, etc. Tests for this course are all supplied by your partner. If your partner has not taken this course, he or she may frequently attempt to help you with your homework. You get extra credit if you respond with gratitude rather than defensiveness. If you begin to improve the way you're living and think you're better than your partner, you get "ego detentions" and are sent to an emergency humility program, where you have to list, on a blackboard in a classroom with no erasers, the most foolish and harmful things you've ever done.

Job Descriptions 202

In this course your work is to change your partner and make him into a better person. The prerequisite for this course is completion of all previous courses with perfect scores and no unfinished assignments.

Unpleasant Emotions and Moods 301

In this course you learn how to accept and handle unpleasant moods and emotions such as anger, frustration, depression, anxiety, grief, and jealousy without blaming your partner or holding him responsible for your feelings. You'll learn an equation for factoring in the trouble you may cause your partner when you consider whether to complain or express unpleasant feelings. You'll develop skills for acting loving, caring, and being patient, even when you don't feel loving, caring, and patient.

Attention 501

This is the advanced course in attention. Notice the ways in which even the gifts you give cause trouble to others. Notice how your helping can be harmful. Notice how the troubles that others cause you are gifts.

Acceptance 302

This course teaches you to accept your partner as an entire life package. It dispels the notion that you can pick and choose what you like and only love the "nice" parts of them while refusing to accept the habits, family members, and physical characteristics that aren't quite so appealing. Your partner (or prospective partner) is a package deal. Take it or leave it. (Note: if you change your mind frequently, life becomes very chaotic.) If you assume you can make some adjustments in the package at a later date, you receive an electric shock every time you touch them with the screwdriver.

* * *

The above are only a few of the courses that are offered. There are many others. Often you don't real-

> "It will always help if each partner asks what way to live is the best way to bring alive the life of the other partner."
> SEIKAN HASEGAWA ROSHI

ize what course you've been taking until it's time for a test. You can drop out of the program at any time by ending the relationship. This is another course and one of the most difficult. One element of this course is that you may have an overwhelming feeling that you'll never find another partner. In time, most of us do. And while we're in between courses, there is always more to learn.

Who Will Do the Laundry?

Reflecting on ourselves must be an ongoing process, and our intimate relationships provide fertile ground. We gain deeper insight into the nature of our relationships, as well as our own nature. How does our awareness change us? How does it change a relationship? Can you solve this riddle?

A husband and wife were having difficulties in their marriage. They each did Naikan for one week. Later, they returned to the Naikan center to have tea with their teacher.

> COUPLE: Before we did the Naikan retreat we always argued about
> who would do the laundry.
> TEACHER: And how is it now?
> COUPLE: Now we always argue about who will do the laundry.
> TEACHER: I'm glad things have improved.

Two Different Worlds

The chart on the facing page shows the contrast between self-centered attention and loving attention to our partner. They are, indeed, two different worlds. How can I be loving toward my part-

SELF-CENTERED ATTENTION	LOVING ATTENTION
How can my partner be more loving?	How can I be more loving?
What am I not getting from my partner?	What am I receiving from my partner?
Taking things for granted	Saying thank you
What troubles is my partner causing me?	What troubles am I causing my partner?
Forgiving my partner	Asking for forgiveness
Changes my partner needs to make	Changes I need to make
Blaming my partner for our problems and difficulties	Seeing my responsibility for our problems and difficulties
Deciding what my partner's goals should be	Supporting the goals my partner has chosen
Noticing my partner's faults and shortcomings	Noticing my own faults and shortcomings
Demanding my rights	Recognizing everything as a gift
"I give so much and receive so little"	"I give so little and receive so much"
What can my partner do for me?	What can I do for my partner?
If he/she really loved me . . .	If I really loved him/her . . .
Our relationship as a vehicle for my happiness	Our relationship as a vehicle for training and learning
My partner should do Naikan reflection	I should do Naikan reflection

ner when I am in the world of self-centered attention? When I am relating to my partner from a self-centered world, I am mostly trying to satisfy my own ego-centered needs. Nothing could be further from love.

Ideally it would be wonderful to respond to others with only loving attention. During those moments when both partners are living in this world, relationships can seem "too good to be true." Yet I must admit to spending the vast majority of my own life in the self-centered column. As I examine myself I am aware of how my laziness and selfishness often dominate my desire to be a loving husband. The right-hand column serves as a reminder of where I would like my attention to be. A reminder that I desperately need. Fortunately, my wife, friends, and teachers are often living reminders of such a place. I am grateful to be surrounded by such people. Without them, I would be quite content to live in a self-centered world under the illusion that I am living somewhere else.

The Practice of Naikan

Without practice, the wisdom derived from self-reflection simply slips away like raindrops running off the roof of a house. In the beginning of this book, I suggested a series of exercises and discussed Naikan's three questions that are the core of Naikan self-reflection:

What have I received from _____?
What have I given to _____?
What troubles and difficulties have I caused _____?

> "Man need only divert his attention from searching for the solution to external questions and pose the one, true inner question of how he should lead his life, and all the external questions will be resolved in the best possible way."
>
> LEO TOLSTOY

The question of troubles others have caused me is conspicuously absent. We are already skilled in this area, and the conduct of others is outside our control. We need no additional practice and Naikan offers us none. It is in the moment-to-moment comprehension of what we receive from others and how we cause them trouble that self-reflection helps us to develop a new self-image and a new way of paying attention.

In this section of the book I offer a more in-depth discussion of Naikan practice, including the Naikan retreat, daily self-reflection, simple exercises, and assignments for holiday celebrations and special occasions.

The Naikan Retreat

Suppose you went away for one week to a small cottage in the mountains. It's quiet and secluded. All your needs are provided for. Your meals are brought to your room. Your laundry and dishes are washed. You're awakened early in the morning and an evening bell tells you it's bedtime. There are no phone calls to answer or bills in the mail. There is no casual chatter and little noise. There is simply silence, a place to sit, and a screen to watch. And on that screen is the story of your life. It's based on a script, but not the revised, edited script you brought with you. No, this is reality's original draft, what really happened. There is nothing to do each day but watch this movie. What would you learn about your life? At the end of the week, when you return home, filled with an expanded knowledge of how you have lived, how will you then live?

What actually happens during a Naikan retreat? Participants

(called *naikansha*) begin by reflecting on their mother, the reflection usually covering from the participant's birth through age six. Participants continue to reflect for three-year periods (ages six to eight, nine to eleven, and so on). In this manner, their entire life can be examined in relation to their mother on a period-by-period basis. Participants then examine the relationship to their father, siblings, spouse, children, teachers, friends, and coworkers. During the retreat, they will have an opportunity to reflect on those with whom tension or resentment has developed because of difficulties in the past. At the end of each period of reflection, usually 90–120 minutes, a staff member meets with the participant to listen to his or her Naikan reflection. The role of the listener (called *mensetsusha* in Japanese) is to listen attentively and suggest the subject for the next period of reflection. Little dialogue takes place, since Naikan is self-reflection, and what there is to be learned is learned by searching and examining one's own direct experience.

Participants are given a small area in which to sit. This area is at least partially enclosed by screens or curtains. Traditionally, participants sit on the floor using cushions, although accommodations can be made for those with back problems or other physical limitations. There is usually a daily work period (twenty minutes), time for a shower, and three meals. Meals are

> "You might wonder if one can really learn anything about oneself in this simple way. But those three questions, because they are so simple, do not leave you any room to get all tangled up in confusing rationalizations. They cause you to strip the self away from its subjectivity and to see objectively."
>
> AKI YAMADA

generally served to participants in their rooms. Otherwise, the entire day, from 5:30 a.m. to 9:30 p.m., is spent in quiet reflection. Talking and reading are discouraged, and telephone calls are only allowed in emergencies. Contact with the outside world is kept to a minimum in order for participants to completely immerse themselves in reflection on their past.

As participants quietly contemplate their lives, the emphasis is on remembering concrete detail rather than generalities. For example, rather than remembering that your mother washed your clothes all the time, you might be more specific, remembering the day you played in a Little League baseball game and your mother woke up early to wash your uniform. Or perhaps there was a day when she picked you up from school when you had chicken pox.

Remembering specific incidents is challenging. It prevents sliding through Naikan reflection with simple statements like "so-and-so was loving" and "so-and-so was very supportive." Such abstract statements are of less value than recollections of detail. Generalizations are concepts; incidents and events actually happened.

Naikan participants are encouraged to spend about 60 percent of their time on the third question, What troubles and difficulties have I caused others? This question is most challenging because relatively little attention has been directed toward it previously. More attention has been focused on how others have caused difficulties. Now participants must look at themselves from the perspective of others.

After several hours of reflection, the Naikan guide comes and gives the participants an opportunity to report on what they have remembered about this period of their life. This meeting (*mensetsu* in Japanese, which also means "interview") may resemble a kind of confession. But it is really just an opportunity for the person to share what they remembered and move on to the next period of reflection. There is no absolution or analysis offered by the guide.

The participant is the sole judge of her own behavior. There is no judgment from outside and no moral code. Defenses are lowered because there is no one to defend against. The participants are free to look, perhaps for the first time, openly and honestly at how they have lived their lives. The person receiving the participant's report simply listens with an open heart, and, when finished, asks the participant to continue to reflect on the next (usually, three-year) period.

Naikan participants are also assigned the topic of lying and stealing (see page 97). Instead of using the three questions listed above, the participants are encouraged to look at their lives, period by period, in order to identify instances in which, broadly interpreted, they lied or stole things. For example, do we lie when we do not honor our commitment to return a library book on time? Do we lie when

> "I believe that I have changed as a result of Naikan, but whether my experience is typical I cannot say. The prime insights have been in realizing my past misdeeds and in seeing what kindnesses I have received from others. I see the latter as most important. I believe that the heart of Naikan is developing a deep appreciation of one's mother, father, siblings, friends and others. To wallow in one's past faults misses something vital. Wallowing is stagnant and destructive. It doesn't compel one toward positive change; a deep appreciation does."
>
> PIERRE D'AMOURS

we exaggerate our talent and skills in a job interview in order to appear to be more competent than we are? Do we steal someone's time when we are ten minutes late for an appointment? Are we stealing when we overhear a conversation that was not meant for our ears? Of course it is not pleasant to recall such transgressions, but they are part of our life history.

Naikan continues until the last hour of the last day. Again and again the participants review their lives in relation to others. When the week is over and it is time to reenter the world, what are the results of such an extraordinary experience?

Interviews and follow-up reports with participants indicate that each person's experience has common threads and unique elements. Nearly everyone interviewed leaves the Naikan center with a strong sense of having been loved and cared for. Resentment and anger toward specific individuals have dissolved in some cases. Former Naikan participants have reported a richness and vibrancy to the world around them that they had seldom known. For some there is a sense of oneness, of connection to the world and to others. Relationships with parents, in particular, are sometimes dramatically changed. Those who entered the retreat with specific problems like alcoholism, criminal behavior, drug addiction, violence, or delinquency (in children) often find the experience of the retreat alleviates or improves their situations significantly. One consistent result of the Naikan experience is a heightened desire to repay others for the many things received from them. The actions by which we give to others, to serve and care for the world around us, transform our real feelings of love and gratitude into real behavior, simultaneously changing us and changing the world around us.

The Naikan retreat can be difficult emotionally and physically. The intensive practice varies somewhat among the centers in Japan. At the Toyama Naikan Center, director Masahiro Nagashima has closely preserved the style of Naikan's founder, Ishin Yoshimoto. At the Senkobo Naikan Center, the style and atmosphere reflect the Rinzai Zen and Pure Land training of Rev. Shue Usami, director of the center's activities. At the Nara Naikan Training Center, psychologist Yoshihiko Miki has created a more clinical environment, reflecting the psychotherapeutic orientation of his, and his wife's, work.

In the Naikan retreat, there is no escape from the investigation of our lives. Participants come face-to-face with their past reality. Other forms of Naikan allow one to do a Naikan exercise and then watch television or read a newspaper. The traditional retreat, however, allows hour-to-hour and day-to-day Naikan with little distraction. It is a rare opportunity for a human being to step back from the business of daily life, reflect on the past, and rethink the direction and meaning of one's existence.

> "This connectedness that I felt, this experience, that I didn't have to protect or defend my little self. I was more connected and I was just me and it's OK to be so limited. I'm usually so overwhelmed by realizing how limited I am. It's just unbearable. I want to be limitless. So for me, I had this extraordinary experience of being absolutely OK, being this limited little person. . . . Therapy tried to help me feel better about myself and all the while the answer for me was to recognize my shortcomings and feel better about the world."
> LUCY APPLETON

Journal Naikan

Many of those who want to do Naikan reflection may find other forms more practical and available. Naikan may be done on a home journal basis, a method used by Professor Akira Ishii of Aoyama Gakuin University in Tokyo. Several periods each week can be devoted to a series of Naikan reflections that are recorded in a journal. It is best if the periods of reflection are at least one hour, although Ishii suggests that it is better not to introduce the pressure of a set time frame. You can begin with reflection on your mother, as is traditional, and then proceed to reflect on your father, followed by other family members, friends, and other important people. If possible, someone with Naikan experience can review the journal periodically. Ishii claims that more than two thousand students have done journal Naikan at his university, and many have found it to be a very meaningful experience. It has also been used in hospital settings with patients whose journals can be reviewed regularly.

Daily Naikan

Daily Naikan (called in Japanese *nichijo naikan*) is a simple and effective way to practice Naikan each evening. Just before going to bed, one spends about thirty minutes reflecting on the day. What was received today and from whom? What was returned to others? And what troubles were caused others? Again, the individual invests at least 60 percent of the time on the third question. I often assign my students daily Naikan each evening for a week as their first introduction to Naikan. Because they are reflecting on the present day, it is easier to remember specific incidents. They can report on their Naikan reflection in a session at the end of the week, or they can report on it the next morning. More recently I have worked with individuals who will send their daily Naikan report by e-mail. An example of daily Naikan is included on page 32.

Daily self-reflection grounds you in the realistic experience of your life, which can often be colored by your feelings or by a single event. For example, your computer may break down and you might feel very frustrated and angry. But during the same day your car worked fine, as did the toaster, the shower, the phone, the stereo, the television, the furnace, and most of the essential organs in your body. When we reflect objectively on these things, we keep ourselves from getting drawn into an emotional stew that gets disconnected from much of our life—the elements of life that reveal the compassion and support we are receiving.

David K. Reynolds has introduced several variations of daily Naikan that may be practiced progressively and reveal different aspects of our daily interactions with life: Do daily Naikan on:

1. people whose faces you know but whose names you do not know (e.g., the bus driver who took you to the subway stop this morning)
2. people whose faces and names you do not know (e.g., the person operating the subway train
3. living nonhumans, such as the cow that provided the milk for your coffee
4. objects such as a car or cassette player (a friend of mine, a professional piano player, did daily Naikan on his piano)
5. forms of energy, such as electricity and heat

Relationship Naikan

Naikan can be an important tool for reflection on our experience with intimate partners and close friends. It can be helpful to married couples who are having difficulty and contemplating divorce or separation. The purpose of Naikan is not to prevent the dissolution of a marriage, but rather to help the individuals see the reality of their relationship so that any decision can be based on facts rather than illusions about themselves and their partners. Individuals are assigned Naikan reflection on their partners, reviewing their marriage in one- or two-year periods, beginning with the time they first met. Over a period of days or weeks they continue their reflection on their partners until they have reached the present day. I encourage those contemplating separation to remain fully involved while they are still together. Not doing so may result in one's regret that the relationship might have been saved if only more had been done. Isn't it better to be more caring and giving and loving while the opportunity is still there? Such a choice isn't necessarily easy, but isn't it wiser? Naikan can be effective as a prescription for troubled relationships, as a means to solve problems that arise by viewing the situation from the other's perspective. Beyond this, the practice of Naikan can prevent certain problems and difficulties from surfacing in the first place. Creating rich soil is at least as important as pulling the weeds.

I have also worked with couples who have done Naikan as preparation for their wedding. In one case a couple scheduled an entire day to reflect on one another as a way of marking the end of one phase of their relationship and the beginning of their life together as husband and wife. The years of this earlier phase were marked by many ups and downs, including drinking problems and unfaithfulness. Their reflection on this time, however, reminded them of the many loving things each partner had given and humbled them as they realized some of their own foolishness and selfishness. In other cases, couples who have been married for many years will use an anniversary as an opportunity to do Naikan reflection and celebrate their marriage.

An exercise I enjoy doing with my wife is bedtime Naikan. As we lie in bed we begin with the first question, What have I received from others today? and alternate answering that question out loud as we reflect on the day. After a while we'll proceed to the second question and then the third. Usually somewhere during the latter two questions, one or both of us falls asleep. During many Naikan retreats I would often try not to fall asleep while doing Naikan, but with bedtime Naikan, I can just allow myself to slowly drift from self-reflection to sleep without any resistance.

Naikan on Parts of the Body

You may wish to try reflecting on parts of your body. For smokers, Naikan reflection on the lungs may be helpful. Photographers may wish to do Naikan reflection on their eyes. What is the reality of the contributions of these valuable parts of the body? A friend of mine had a painful toothache last month. She had to go through several days of discomfort before it could be treated and the pain subsided. What a wonderful thing it is not to have a toothache! How kind of the world to give us days of comfort such that the teeth go unnoticed. There is a Zen saying, "When the shoe fits we forget the foot."

Perhaps it is worth taking a moment to thank your teeth for so many moments of service. What have you done for your teeth? Have you neglected them? Is there something you can do to repay them? Notice the way in which Naikan reflection may affect the treatment and care we give to our bodies.

Naikan Exercises

There are a number of exercises that stimulate a Naikan-inspired awareness in our daily lives. During my training in Japan I was asked to consider the financial give-and-take between my parents and me. First, I was asked to calculate the amount of money my parents spent on me from before my birth until my twenty-first birthday. I had to consider the cost of clothing, medical care, school supplies, toys, piano lessons, food, and, of course, my share of the rent, utilities, car expenses, insurance, etc. I tried to estimate these expenses with as much attention to detail as possible. Then I was asked to calculate how much I spent on them during that same period of time.

This number was disappointingly low. Even the small gifts I bought for birthdays and Christmas often came from the allowance they gave me. I worked during my teens, but I used the money to have fun with my friends and perhaps set aside a little for college. Later, I was asked to make a similar comparison for my adult years. How much did they spend on me since age twenty-one? How much did I spend on them? I would have expected more parity between these figures, but I was wrong. As I grew older my "receipts" grew at a much faster pace than my "payments."

Here are some additional exercises that promote self-reflection and that can be integrated into one's daily life:

1. Throughout the day, when someone does something for you, say a "mindful thank-you." Do this by saying thank you and then identifying the act for which you are expressing appreciation. For example, "Thank you for opening the door" or "Thank you for pouring me some orange juice." We can easily get into the habit of saying "thank you" mindlessly: we say the words but pay little attention to what is/was actually done for us. A mindful thank-you requires an extra pause to pay attention and consider what we are receiving from the other person.

2. Prior to each bite at mealtime, silently thank one person or thing that contributed to the meal. For example, thank the farmer who grew the corn, thank the soil, thank the truck driver who delivered the corn to the store. This is also a great way to slow down your pace if you tend to eat quickly, as I do.

3. Garbage Naikan is an exercise in which you take a moment to thank something as you are about to throw it away. What have you received from it? How has it served you? For example, you might thank the tissue for wiping the tears from your eyes. Or the plastic wrapper for keeping a piece of chocolate fresh. Are there services from these objects that you have been taking for granted?

4. David Reynolds suggests a Constructive Living exercise in which we clean out a drawer and thank each item as we reorganize the space and return it to its home. This can make us more aware of the service of objects such as socks, tools, utensils, etc.

Reporting Our Naikan Reflections

Reporting the results of our self-reflection is important, as confirmed by my own experiences and those of my students. We tend mostly to try to show others the good things we have done and keep the bad things a secret. So we go through life creating an image of ourselves that is not very realistic. Our transgressions, mistakes, and self-centered behavior are also part of the reality of our lives. When we acknowledge this reality to another, we are more honest about ourselves and we relieve some of the pressure to "look good" to others. It is good to report your reflections to someone who has experience doing Naikan themselves. Some people present their Naikan reflections to God, Buddha, Allah, or some higher power. Other people share their recollections with a partner or family member. Still others reflect silently and do not report their Naikan reflection to anyone. At the other end of the communication is the listener. Listening to someone who has sincerely reflected on his or her life is a privilege and can be a very meaningful experience. When we listen we should do so humbly, as if we were receiving an important gift from an honored friend or hearing a sacred story from a wise person.

Across from me are a pair of hands pressed against the floor. The palm of the right hand is flat against the floor and the palm of the left hand is similarly placed, while slightly overlapping its counterpart. I notice the

> **"I have been blessed by this experience [Naikan retreat] to see reality, and now can make decisions on how to live my life better by seeing the consequences of my actions. So now I start my journey, again. . . ."**
>
> LAURA LICATO

knuckles and the texture of the skin. Sometimes the nails are bitten, sometimes long, sometimes neatly trimmed. There may be a twitch or an itch; here and there a tap. Each set of hands is unique. Each is attached to a human being. A human being who has freely chosen to look at the reality of her life. A human being who does me the honor of allowing me to listen. Whether painful or joyful, this person's life is her life. And those moments in which I receive a glimpse of it are precious and sacred.

I know a lot about her hands because it is the only part of her I see as she reports her Naikan reflection. At the beginning of a Naikan retreat, participants are asked to keep their eyes lowered and to avoid eye contact with others. Naikan is about introspection. It's about examining our own lives. There is no room for looking at others. We look at ourselves.

The person across from me reports on her Naikan. She begins by reporting what she has received from the subject of her reflection. Sometimes the list is long. Sometimes she remembers very little. Periodically I can hear a note of revelation in her voice, as if to say, "Oh my goodness, I never really considered this before." Then she moves on to report what she has given or returned to the other person. Often these lists are disappointingly short. "I must have given more than that!" the inner voice says regretfully.

Some of the things we have given are, well, curious. Arthur says he gave joy to his parents by stopping his drinking. Sheila says she saved her husband money by not spending as much as she might have. Jill says she gave her secretary a lot of work so she wouldn't be bored. These are gifts worthy of further examination. What did I receive in order to give these gifts? Could the things I gave have caused the other person trouble? What was I considering when I gave these gifts? Was I really doing it for them? How did I benefit from what I gave or did? More questions, more discoveries.

Finally comes the list of troubles. These memories are the most difficult to report. One by one she reports ways she has caused the other person difficulty and suffering. Jennifer remembers slapping her little sister when she had to baby-sit on a Friday night. Steven remembers using his ex-wife's inheritance to gamble on horse races. Moments of tears. Moments of guilt. Incredible courage. More truth excavated and uncovered.

I'm on my knees with my head bowed, just listening. At times their comments remind me of my own Naikan reflection. I remember the care I received. I remember ways I have caused suffering and harm to others. I remember how selfish I've been and how little I've given. In spite of all my selfishness and harmful ways, life has cared for me like a mother caring for her newborn baby. Not because I earned it or deserved it. Not because I am a good person. But because life's compassion and care penetrate my own life in infinite ways.

As one of life's representatives, I try to open my heart to this human being who has the courage to search for truth and see reality as it is. But if and when my heart opens, I know it is not my doing.

The participant announces she is finished; she has nothing more to report. I bow and say thank you. I have nothing else to offer her. No absolution, no forgiveness, no analysis, or even comfort. I have no magic to hand out. The magic is already within her. The magic is in the space between the question and the answer. The magic brings the question. The magic is the desire to know the magic.

As I stand, I thank this woman for her cushion. She places it in my spot prior to each interview, her apparent response to having noticed my discomfort in kneeling on the wood floor. Even as I sit and listen, the world supports me, literally, turning hardness into softness.

Holidays: Opportunities for Reflection and Celebration

In our society, we seem to have lost sight of the meaning of many holidays. Too often, a holiday is an excuse for a day away from work, for eating enormous quantities of unhealthy food, for watching sporting events drowned in commercials, and for buying and giving unnecessary consumer products. Many of these holidays have the potential to be periods where we step back and reflect on our lives, days in which we celebrate something more profound than a new toaster or victory for the home team. But to find deeper meaning in the holidays requires us to radically rethink our habitual behavior. How can we redesign the activities of these days to stimulate personal reflection, service to others, and more mindful approaches to celebration?

In this section I would like to introduce you to ways in which you can integrate self-reflection into some of our holiday celebrations—New Year's, Thanksgiving, Mother's Day. The possibilities go far beyond this short list. Earlier in the book I mentioned weddings and anniversaries as opportunities for Naikan reflection. Many of the same ideas I mention about Mother's Day will apply to Father's

Day as well. Independence Day can also be thought of as Interdependence Day, and Memorial Day as the spring equinox—even my birthday has a different meaning as I have come to see these occasions from a much different perspective. Rather than be put to sleep by alcohol or hypnotized by television, these are days for waking up.

Holidays. Holy days.

Naikan for the New Year

How will you spend the last day of this year? For a few years a group of us gathered at Barbara's home on December 31st to reflect on our lives. We would reflect for up to twelve hours leading to the first moment of the new year. We would consider the gifts, support, and care we received from so many people and objects during the past year. Then we would celebrate with one another, sharing our good fortune of the past and our goals for the coming year.

We would set up one room as a "receiving room," where any of the participants could go to share their Naikan reflection. Experienced participants would take turns staying in this room and listening to the Naikan reflection of others.

Last year I sat in the corner of a basement, sitting on a cushion and staring at a wall. Periodically the furnace would go on and my mind would alternate between moments of frustration at the whir of the motor and moments of gratitude for the heat I was receiving that kept me warm during a rather frigid evening.

> **"The years teach much which the days never know"**
> RALPH WALDO EMERSON

New Year's is a good time to identify goals for the coming year. If we are graced with another year of life, how can we make the most of this time? How can we best serve the world? Can we begin to repay, in some small way, those who have been so caring and supportive during the past year—during our entire life?

As a New Year's exercise, try making a list of ten of the most important people in your life. For each person, reflect on the three most important things they have done for you or given to you. Notice how many of these items were important, not just in their own right, but had led to other wonderful experiences and opportunities that may not otherwise have occurred. Then ask yourself, "What can I give to this person, or do for this person, in the coming year?" Try to select something that would be important from their perspective rather than something you think would be good for them. Eventually, the list is completed: ten gifts or services for ten personal supporters who have attended to us.

When you complete your list, make it your goal to give each gift or service in the coming year. Add this goal to your other goals. Place it on top of your list. What could be more important? It may not pay off your debts, or make adequate amends for the troubles you have caused, but those who have supported us deserve some act of gratitude, some tangible sign of appreciation, a few moments of our undivided attention.

Realistically, what can we give? We function merely as agents and delivery people. Objects and services pass through us as gifts are transferred and distributed from one point of the universe to another. Each stop is temporary. Gifts just can't sit still. Life caring for itself, serving itself, and constantly rearranging itself.

It's almost midnight now. Our formal reflection ends and we quietly begin to warm the bounty of food brought by the participants. I always look forward to the vegetarian shepherd's pie Julie brings. She travels hundreds of miles from Washington, D.C., to be here for just one night. At midnight we eat and celebrate the ending of one year and the beginning of another. Then we gradually find a quiet little spot and drift off to sleep. And that furnace with the noisy motor keeps me warm all night. Even though I'm not awake.

Suggestions for New Year's Naikan Reflection

Listed below are many Naikan-related exercises you can do to begin the new year. In our quiet reflection we can experience a different kind of New Year's celebration. We can celebrate the gifts of our lives. We can toast the kindness others have shown to us. We can get drunk on the love we have received in spite of our own limitations and mistakes.

1. Reflect on your mother, father, or other people who have supported you during the past year. You may have received things during an earlier time period, but still benefited from them during the past year.

2. Do Naikan reflection on someone with whom you've had difficulty, conflict, or tension during the past year. This is often the type of self-reflection we don't feel like doing. Maybe that is an indication that it is needed.

3. Make a list of one hundred things you've received this past year without providing any compensation or consideration. These could be things you received as gifts, things you stole, or things you used without payment.

4. Make a list of twenty-five important services that were done

for you during the past year.

5. Reflect on ways you caused trouble and difficulty to the people you listed in exercise number 4, above.

6. Reflect on your lying and stealing for the past year.

7. Reflect on your speech this past year. In what ways have you spoken critically, harmfully, or inappropriately about others. How did this cause harm or trouble?

8. Reflect on ways you mistreated objects during the past year.

9. What have you learned this past year? Who taught you? Make a list of all the people and objects that helped you to learn and grow, personally, professionally, and spiritually.

10. Write thank-you letters to those who have cared for you and served you this past year.

Thanksgiving

I think it's wonderful we have a holiday called Thanksgiving. But I'm afraid that for many families Thanksgiving Day is no longer infused with the spirit that could make it a wonderful day of gratitude and grace.

If a foreign exchange student were to spend her first Thanksgiving holiday with an American family, what would her experience be? Perhaps she would write home to her parents:

Dear Mom and Dad,

I was looking forward to celebrating this holiday they have in the U.S. called Thanksgiving. Originally I thought it was a wonderful idea. As the day began, the children spent the morning playing video games and watching TV. In the afternoon people

> **"Today is for-giving."**
> PATRICIA RYAN MADSON

drank beer and wine, and then we had a huge meal. I've never seen so much food. But, Mom, you wouldn't believe how much of it was wasted, enough to feed a family in our village for a week. During the meal people complained about their lives and talked about their problems. They criticized many of the relatives who weren't in attendance, and Lisa's dad got into a big argument with her uncle. Later in the day the kids played outside while most of the men watched a game called football on TV. Mostly, the day was like a big party. I'm not sure why they call this holiday Thanksgiving.

I believe it is time for a Thanksgiving revolution. We must make a sincere effort to recapture the spirit of this day. Shouldn't some time be spent reflecting on our life, on what we have received, and giving thanks for those blessings? I'd like to suggest some alternatives—food for thought—to the more conventional ways of observing Thanksgiving Day. Let's begin by creating some guidelines for what we won't include in our celebration:

No complaining.
No criticism of others.
No television, video games, or using computers.
No eating/killing of animals.
No wasting of food.
No alcohol.

Many people might agree with "no complaining" and "no criticism" But perhaps you associate Thanksgiving with turkey and cannot envision a holiday table without a cooked bird as the centerpiece. Maybe you find it relaxing to watch the football game or enjoy a glass of wine with dinner.

Thanksgiving Blessing

We give thanks for the food that gives us life and for the beings that have died so that we might continue to live.

We give thanks for the cars and planes and roads that allow us to be together on this day.

We give thanks for whatever health remains in these temporary bodies of ours.

We give thanks for this shelter that keeps us warm and dry even while we sleep.

We give thanks for our jobs that help us pay for what we need to live.

We give thanks to our parents who brought us into this world.

We give thanks for the mysterious force that keeps our heart beating and life flowing through our bodies.

We vow to wake up, to live each day fully, to see reality as it is, and to use our life for the purpose for which it was intended.

So what shall we do all day instead? Well, let's begin the morning with a period of quiet reflection or meditation. This gives us a chance to step back from our lives and think about our good fortune before we get too busy. There are so many things I don't appreciate when I am busy. One of the benefits of not being busy is that it creates a window for gratitude and the awareness of life's blessings.

During our quiet time we will make a list of these blessings. Some may be obvious, like a house, a car, or good health. But others will only surface after we begin searching with the flashlight of our consciousness. For example, we might become aware of the gift of being able to send and receive mail. We complain when the post office raises the price of a stamp, but isn't it amazing that we can send a letter to a friend thousands of miles away for only pennies?

After we have had some quiet time in the morning, we'll write some thank-you letters. For example:

Dear Mailperson,

Thank you for delivering my mail to me approximately 285 times this year. I seldom get to see you and mention how convenient it is to have mail brought directly to my home each day. I know my dog barks every time you walk up to the front porch. I guess you're used to it by now. Still, it must be a bit disconcerting to be walking around all day delivering mail and then you're greeted by ferocious barks instead of a smile or word of gratitude. Sorry about that. I know there were many days when you probably didn't feel like delivering the mail. But you came anyway. Though some of my mail was not particularly useful, some of it was quite important—money, important letters from overseas, valuable documents. Thank you for being such a reliable link between me and the rest of the world.

After we've written some thank-you notes, we might get together with everybody and share some of the things we're thankful for. It's a wonderful way to launch into the more active part of the day.

And what about the food we eat? Is it really a good idea to express gratitude by killing and devouring a beautiful, majestic bird like the turkey? We often see wild turkeys browsing around the yard of our home in Vermont. I understand that Benjamin Franklin suggested that we make the turkey our national bird instead of the eagle. Let's instead adopt a turkey through a program such as that offered by Farm Sanctuary in Watkins Glen, New York (1-888-SPONSOR). Two hundred years ago it was necessary to kill animals like turkeys in order to survive. But nowadays we can have a delicious meal without killing these lovely birds.

But if we don't have turkey, then what will we eat? How about fish? Well, they're also living creatures. I assume they find it unpleasant and painful to be killed. How about vegetables? Sorry, also living things that will die so that we can eat and live. Whatever we choose to eat, we need to reconsider our attitude toward food. Instead of, "Let's dig in and eat until we bust," we should apologize to our food:

> I'm sorry sweet potatoes and cranberries for eating you and ending your life on this planet. Please forgive me. I am a selfish creature who needs the nourishment you have to offer in order to continue my own life. I will try not to waste you or take more of you than I truly need. Thanks for keeping me alive. I'm sorry I cannot do the same for you.

Another change we can make for Thanksgiving is to expand our circle of celebration beyond our family. Many people, including children and seniors, have no families to join for Thanksgiving. Let's make a special effort to seek out those outside our families and have them join our celebration.

Now that we've addressed the "thanks" side of this holiday, let's look at the "giving" side. We can use the day to exchange gifts. They wouldn't have to be store-bought gifts. We'll bring something we already own that we want to give away. Not because it's broken or useless, but because it's valuable and we'd like someone else to enjoy it for a while. We'll also do some kind of community service—cleaning up the local playground, painting the fence at the local library, even picking up trash on the street. Perhaps for the birds we'll scatter some extra seed. Maybe we'll write a letter for Amnesty International on behalf of some political prisoner who doesn't have the luxury of picking up trash on the street.

Once we have put the "thanks" and the "giving" back into this holiday, let's consider expanding Thanksgiving beyond one solitary day in November. Why not give the other months an equal share of gratitude and thanks? What about a monthly Thanksgiving Day? Or an entire week of Thanksgiving rather than just one day?

So please consider joining this revolution. What will help you and your family reclaim the true spirit of Thanksgiving? What can you do on this special day to ignite the fire of gratitude and awaken your heart to the endless stream of gifts that support your life each day?

Let Thanksgiving be a day for waking up. For remembering. Noticing. Thanking. Giving.

Mother's Day

"Mother, you never bothered to tell me you loved me. You never loved me for myself. You just wanted me to fulfill your own unfulfilled dreams. You weren't there for me when I needed you. You only paid attention to me when I got good grades in school."

These comments are characteristic of those of us who have

searched the depths of our souls to get in touch with our anger at our mothers, encouraged by an army of talk-show hosts, authors, recovery programs, and therapists, all helping us to take an *honest* look at our childhoods and then take aim at our moms. Of course, we'll take time out on Mother's Day to send a card, make a phone call, or offer a small gift to the woman who, among other things, brought us into the world. But this small detail, and many others, are lost or forgotten amidst an array of people and programs who see mom as just another casualty on the road to self-realization and self-esteem.

Of course, mothers aren't perfect. They make mistakes. They make foolish choices. They act selfishly and lose their temper. Some of them abandon and abuse their children. But before we abandon them, it might be wise to review the record.

My first serious attempt to do that came in 1989 when I spent two weeks at a Naikan center near Kuwana, Japan, reflecting on my entire life. For

"When I was in the fourth grade I was put in a class for gifted kids that was started at my elementary school. They brought in kids from all over the city, but I was the only kid from Lawrence Elementary who was put in the class. So all my old friends were in a different classroom. And then the school had us compete with the other class—in softball, academics, etc. I was miserable and tried to get out of the class to be with my old friends. So good old mom started up a Girl Scout troop so I could at least be with my old friends after school. She took us on field trips and camping trips and sat up all night one time with her assistant when she had asthma and couldn't sleep."

BECKY WINNING

more than a day I did nothing but reflect on my relationship with my mother, year by year. What had she given me during my childhood? Memories came slowly at first, and were somewhat vague. But from time to time a vivid image would surface of her making me a bologna and cheese sandwich for my lunch box, or washing my muddy Little League baseball uniform, or sitting down and playing the piano with me. Some of my reflections on my mom involved calculations: How many times did she change my dirty diapers? How many meals did she cook for me? How many loads of laundry did she wash? These images and vignettes aren't full of drama like those often found in therapists' offices or on talk shows. Folding laundry can be pretty tedious when you're doing it, and perhaps even more tedious when you're simply thinking about somebody else doing it. Much of what is required of mothers is not exciting: laundry, dishes, diapers, sitting on a playground bench and watching your son climb up and down monkey bars. It is precisely because of the undramatic nature of these services that they are overlooked, forgotten, or taken for granted. They don't get discussed in therapy. They aren't a common subject of self-help books. They don't appear as a central theme in the TV sitcom. But when we reflect on our lives and our relationship to our moms, it's essential to remember these acts of service for one very important reason: they happened.

By the time I completed my two-week stay at the Naikan center, my relationship with my mom was forever changed. It's not that I became a model son or built her a home on the Riviera. It's just that my memory was a bit more complete and my image of her was different. I could rarely talk with her on the phone without remembering some of the excavated memories from Japan. And those memories included my own mistreatment of her as a child and adolescent. They included my own ingratitude toward her for what she had done for me.

Now that I am married I have a chance to witness my wife caring for my daughter in many of the same ways I was cared for. It's a kind of déjà vu Naikan reflection on my own mother. And my father. Now that I am on the other end, I have a much better sense of what kind of energy, time, inconvenience, and love it takes to care for a child who is completely dependent on the world for everything. Come to think of it, that's still a pretty good description of me. The mother that raised me lives far away, but her role has been assumed by others, by my wife, my friends, my teachers, the supermarket, the garden, the people who make fresh apple cider down the road, and the person I call when I can't get the computer to work. I'm still mothered. I'm still cared for. But there was one woman who got me started as a seedling and made sure I was firmly rooted until I could transplant myself. She deserves to be remembered for all the tedious, unexciting things she did for me. As my way of honoring your service, Mom, I plan to fold some laundry today.

A Mother's Day Letter

Dear Mom,

I hope this letter finds you doing well and that your back is feeling a bit better. I'm thankful to have the opportunity to see you next week—a delayed Mother's Day meeting—and I look forward to my visit.

I have enclosed a picture of some beautiful baby robins in a nest by our garden taken last spring. It was a wonderful experience to find the three soft-blue eggs and watch them hatch one by one. I would go up to the nest and make a squeaky bird sound and they would pop up their heads and open their mouths. They reminded me so much of myself. They couldn't yet see, but their automatic reaction was to think only of what they wanted. Their mother and father cared for them diligently, searching for food and bringing it back for the children. I doubt these robins were as difficult children as I was, but it wasn't long until they were strong enough to fly away on their own. Perhaps they are building a nest this spring and raising their own family.

At the time I left for college at age seventeen I mostly felt relief. I wanted to get out of the house more than anything in the world. Maybe the robins felt the same way. It took me many years to begin to understand the love and care that you provided me when I was younger. I looked at the little robins and realized that I was just as helpless as they were. I survived and became healthy in our home/nest because I was so well cared for. Though you seldom, maybe never, received a word of thanks, you cooked for me, cleaned house for me, bought and washed my clothes for me, arranged for me to take music lessons, and went to work for me. Mostly you heard complaints or I made noise when I wanted something I didn't have.

Thank you for your patience, love, and care for those first seventeen years of my life. Thank you for making sure I had food when I came home from basketball practice. Thank you for encouraging me to take piano lessons and practice. All of your concrete efforts became part of me. When I write an essay, give a lecture, or plant flowers, you are with me doing those things. When I smile at a beautiful sunset or make a dinner salad, you are part of that experience. Much of my own genetic makeup that provided me with a healthy body comes from you and your parents. Perhaps this realization was more clear when I first emerged from your body. But it is no less a fact today, even though my own nest is many miles away.

I continue to be well cared for and I have a very fortunate life. Life has taken over where you left off, and I receive food, shelter, clothing, sunsets, fresh air and water, a lovely wife and dog, and the grace to appreciate all this when I'm not so wrapped up in what I want that I'm not getting. Like these little birds, it's hard to open my eyes when my mouth is always reaching for more. Thank you for making my life possible and for being a part of it.

I wish you a heartfelt happy Mother's Day. Thanks to the airplane, pilots, mechanics, engineers, factory workers, travel agents, traffic controllers, flight attendants, cooks, welders, electricians, and thousands of others, I'll be able to visit you next week. How kind of them to bring us together again. Having never learned to fly, I remain, forever, dependent on others.

All my love,
Your son

Self-Reflection and Service

Christians speak of God's love and Pure Land Buddhists refer to the "grace" or vow of Amida Buddha. The practice of Naikan does not deny or assert the existence of such omnipotent beings. It focuses on the actual manifestations of compassion, love, and grace. To that extent it provides a concrete foundation for the devoted Christian, Buddhist, Muslim, Jew, and Hindu, as well as the agnostic. The evidence of some higher power is on display, but each of us must search for the source.

> "To receive everything one must open one's hands and give."
> **TAISEN DESHIMARU ROSHI**

In devoting ourselves to a supreme being our attention may be placed on the spiritual source of support to such an extent that we fail to notice the reality of how that support is manifested in daily life. While we are busy "believing in" the spirit of the tree, we fail to notice the fruit and shade that are given each day. In noticing the fruit and shade our gratitude for the tree is nourished, and this nourishment can inspire us to nourish others.

The support and compassion of the world surround us in each moment of our lives. Even as we sleep, a bed provides us with comfort, a blanket keeps us warm, and a roof keeps us dry. And conversely, when we care for something, when we water a plant, walk a dog, or write a kind letter, are we not extensions of this same power? So we are not only surrounded by love, support, and compassion but we are also vehicles for others to be similarly surrounded. The love, support, and compassion of the universe cannot exist without its representatives, and nothing exists that does not potentially represent such universal love.

Albert Schweitzer said,

> We are gripped by God's will of love, and must help carry out
> that will in this world, in small things as in great things, in saving
> as in pardoning. To be glad instruments of God's love in this
> imperfect world is the service to which we are called.

To produce shade on a sunny day without pride or boast; that is the nature of a tree. How extraordinary! How do we discover our own true nature, our unique role in the web of life, without adding the condiments of pride and arrogance?

Boat-i-sattvas

In New York harbor you can witness a demonstration of service and compassion embodied in little mechanical sea creatures. I call them Boat-i-sattvas, derived from the Buddhist term *bodhisattva*. Bodhisattvas are beings of great wisdom and compassion who dedicate themselves to serving and helping others, resembling, in some ways, Christian saints. It is said that they voluntarily turn away from the gates of Nirvana in order to assist others along the path to Nirvana. But the little water-traveling Boat-i-sattvas I am talking about are not mystical, religious beings. They are powerful little seagoing vessels commonly referred to as tugboats.

Their mission is to help other vessels. That is their purpose in life. They scurry up and down, in and around the harbor in order to assist other vessels in need. They help cruise liners, freighters, and tankers to dock. They tow barges filled with garbage. They assist floating cranes. They escort some ships coming in from the ocean and escort others out. They even help each other out when they get into trouble. They do all this in every kind of weather. Snowstorms, freezing rainstorms, and gale winds are obstacles but not deterrents from their work. Many tugboats work twenty-four hours a day. They carry two crews that sleep in alternating shifts so they can remain ready for the next call for help.

They make their work look easy, almost effortless. There is a special type of beauty in the character of those who can make pulling a 50,000-ton ship appear effortless. How can such small creatures provide guidance and support for those who are so much larger? The answer is in their

> "Unless individuals have given some form of service, I believe that it will be difficult for them to feel that life is ultimately fulfilling."
>
> PATCH ADAMS, M.D.

strength and their wisdom. Their strength comes from their engine, and they are nearly all engine. Most of the ships they assist carry a great deal of cargo and baggage. But the Boat-i-sattvas carry no baggage of their own. When you have rid yourself of your own baggage, it is easier to help others carry theirs. Pound for pound, they are more powerful than the largest of cargo ships. Their wisdom comes from the experience of their small crews. They know the territory. They know where the channel is deepest and where it is shallow. They know the currents and the tides. You can read about these things in books, but their wisdom does not come from books, it comes from the direct experience of life. The elegance with which they push and tow is a product of their strength and wisdom.

Their work is by no means easy, nor is it safe. Tugboats can easily sink. There is little distance between the deck of the boat and the water, so they can easily be pulled under. They have no watertight compartments like most larger ships. In responding to the difficulties of others, those difficulties become their own, and their own welfare and safety are jeopardized.

In 1966, two tankers collided in New York harbor. One was loaded with naphtha, a highly flammable petroleum product. Boat-i-sattvas from all over the harbor came to help. The naphtha was pouring out of a hole in the tanker's bow, and when it ignited, the ship and surrounding water burst into flames. Dozens of tugboats maneuvered through the burning water to pick up crew members who had jumped from the flaming ship. One tugboat, the *Esse Vermont,* was trapped by the flames and exploded. Her entire crew was killed. But many sailors were rescued by the courageous little tugs.

The tugs then managed to separate the tankers and pull them away from shore, where an explosion would have ignited an oil storage facility only 250 yards away.

One of the tugboats that participated in the rescue, the *Julia C. Moran,* was later awarded the Gallant Ship Award by the U.S. Department of Commerce. But that is unusual. Most of the efforts of Boat-i-sattvas go unrecognized and unrewarded. They quietly arrive, do their job, and then go on to the next ship. And sometimes, in between ships, there is a bird, dog, or human being to pull out of the water.

The most surprising thing I've discovered about tugboats is the way they've impacted on my own life. Most large cargo boats can't dock without the assistance of a tug. They're too large and bulky, and as they slow down, the ability to steer them vanishes altogether. So the tugboat plays an essential role in allowing the cargo to reach its destination. That cargo includes foreign-made cars from Japan and Europe, bananas from Central America, and oil from the Middle East. It includes clothing and electronic items from Hong Kong and wool from New Zealand. Many of our imported goods come by ship, and most ships, at one point or another, are guided and pushed and pulled by these little Boat-i-sattvas.

So now when I cross New York harbor on the Staten Island Ferry and I notice a little tugboat off in the distance, I can't help but smile. Sometimes I even wave. If members of the crew see me at all they probably think I'm just saying hello, but really I'm saying thank you. I have come to respect and admire those little vessels who have become my teachers. They teach without words. As I watch them it reminds me how I am towed, pushed, pulled, and guided through the straits and channels of life. Boat-i-sattvas: you can't always see them, but they're always there.

Genza, the Myokonin

Tenko Nishida was a spiritual leader in Japan at the beginning of the twentieth century. He taught people about humility and service to others. He and his followers would often be found cleaning public toilets, a job considered to be one of the lowest and dirtiest jobs one could do. In 1923 he gave a lecture in a mountain village in Tottori Prefecture. A peasant named Genza from a nearby village had intended to hear the lecture but missed his train. By the time he arrived, the lecture had just ended.

When Tenko heard of Genza's ill fortune, he said to him, "I hear you have come a long way to hear what I had to say. I am sorry."

"It is you who have come a long distance to talk to us. You must be tired. Let me massage you," replied Genza.

As Genza massaged Tenko's shoulders, he inquired as to the subject of the evening talk.

"You know that as we grow older we are apt to get impatient and so we must suppress our anger and sympathize with other people, for they too have their own troubles," said Tenko.

Genza replied, "To this day, I have never condoned others, for I am the one who has been condoned without my knowing it."

Tenko didn't quite understand Genza's comment, so he asked him to explain. Genza said softly, "I have never been in a position to forgive others because I was always wrong. I was the one to be forgiven."

Tenko, it is said, was quite taken by this explanation. Even the man whose life embodied the ideals of service and humility was startled by the response of the simple and unassuming peasant. When I heard this story, I also was startled, startled as I realized how often my mind works so differently from Genza's. Rather than examine myself, I commonly justify or rationalize my behavior. For example, my diet has changed over the years, but no matter how it has changed I always think I have the "right" diet. About people who eat less healthy foods, I think, "They should eat better. They are not taking care of their bodies." I think such things even though I had that same type of diet for many years. As for people who eat more healthful foods than I do, I think they are inflexible or unnecessarily extreme in their lifestyle. What a contrast these thoughts are to Genza's simple and humble "I was always wrong."

In this story Genza is a *myokonin*, a Japanese term used to describe the most devoted followers of Pure Land Buddhism. It is sometimes translated as "wonderfully good man." Unlike the wise, courageous "heroes" of the other sects, *myokonin* are often peasants whose lives are testimony to faith, humility, and simplicity.

Wicker in the Wind
BY NICK CALLIE

Outside on a sunny day with a mild wind blowing, I was asked to spray paint a rather weather-worn wicker basket designed to hold a potted plant. Shaking the can to mix the paint with the propellant and feeling the wind blowing against me, the thought came into mind to check the direction of the wind. I made a short test spray to make sure that, while I was painting the basket, the wind would not be painting me.

Placing the basket on its side, on top of the picnic table, I directed the spray inside to paint the bottom, then spraying down, painted the inner sides, spraying and rotating until it looked as if the entire inside had been covered. Turning the basket upright and repeating the process with an occasional shake of the can, I continued until the outer side was completed. Making a mental note that the paint was absorbed rather quickly, I waited only a few moments before again placing the basket on its side and painted the bottom. I had sprayed top to bottom and back, side to side as well, and, feeling rather satisfied with a job well done, stood back to admire my good work.

The wind blew with one strong gust and blew the basket off the table and into the grass and leaves below. Reaching down and picking up the basket, I turned it around and surveyed it for any debris that may have stuck to the wet paint. The fall had jarred the wicker just enough to shift the loose weave, and before my eyes were what appeared to be hundreds of unpainted spots the spray had never reached. Feeling more aggressive I picked up the paint can, shook it very energetically, and, holding it firmly in my hand like a weapon aimed at my target, I let out an audible gasp of breath as I heard the air leaving the can and looked to see that I had run out of paint. . . .

"That man should receive God in himself is good, and by this reception he is a virgin. But that God should become fruitful in him is better; for the fruitfulness of a gift is the only gratitude for the gift."

MEISTER ECKHART

In Appreciation

Nick Callie was one of my first students, dedicating himself to the action

(Morita Therapy) and reflection (Naikan) components of Constructive Living. He worked as hard in his training as anyone I know. He wrote the above essay after a one-day event entitled "A Day of Mindful Living." It's a day when we all attempt to bring a quality of mindfulness and attention to everything we do.

In July 1990 Nick Callie died. I continue to benefit from several important gifts I received from him. He designed the artwork for my audiotape program, *Doing a Good Job,* and he designed my stationery with a distinctive Morita/Naikan logo. He was a talented artist and a challenging student who taught me much.

The wicker basket Nick spray painted sits in my living room next to my meditation cushion. Shortly after it was painted, I placed a small plant in the basket. The plant has flourished as it drinks up the sunlight, water, and air, finding support for its life from the basket Nick repaired. Nick's death reminds me that I, too, will "run out of paint." I will experience that last gasp of breath and this body I am borrowing will be emptied forever. And so Nick's essay, and life and death, are an inspiration to me. An inspiration to live life fully and attentively. An inspiration to try and give myself away in what I do. An inspiration to use the paint that remains in my own can to try to renew little pieces of the world as some small payment for the life that I am still fortunate enough to retain. Thank you, Nick, for all that you have done. You live on in what you have given away.

Perspectives

Many years ago I had an opportunity to travel to New York City to teach and work with students. I generally stayed on Staten Island

and would take the ferry across the Hudson River to Manhattan. It's a lovely ride that goes right past the Statue of Liberty. I could have my breakfast on the boat while I watched Staten Island shrink and change in the distance. I would look back and remember that only minutes ago I was waiting for the bus to take me to the ferry. Staten Island didn't really seem like an island then. It was just a place that was under and all around me. There was no indication that it had a shape and was surrounded by water. But now that I look back I can see what I couldn't see at the time. Now that I have some distance, I can understand a little bit more about Staten Island.

At the other end of my trip was Manhattan, also an island. As we got closer to Manhattan, the buildings began to grow; they got larger and I began to see more details of style and shape. But just about six minutes before we would dock at the lower end of Manhattan, a strange thing would happen. The island of Manhattan would begin to rotate. Have you ever seen an island rotate? It's extraordinary! Everything changes and shifts, and you can see things you never saw before. Buildings that were previously hidden suddenly begin to appear. They were always there, but their existence was obstructed by the larger buildings in front. Yet now I could see them. In some cases an entire building became visible. In others, just the edges of a building could be seen, still partially obstructed but a reality nonetheless. Even the large buildings that I could see all along were changing. I began to see their sides or backs. Many new details became visible. There is much to learn when an island rotates right in front of your eyes.

This all happened because the boat I was on took a sharp turn to the east. That's all that needs to be done to rotate an entire island, actually an entire world: a great feat of magic accomplished by a simple little turn. If we stand in the same spot we may notice something new, something different. But the angle is the same. If we are willing to move slightly, we gain the power to rotate an entire world. And what is revealed may be astonishing.

Even if we go back to the original spot, we can never forget what we saw.

Final Reflection

I wrote the above essay ten years before the tragedy that destroyed the World Trade Center and caused the death of thousands of people on September 11, 2001. The essay refers to islands, but there are no islands, only the single, interconnected web of life. The essay refers to the Statue of Liberty, but there is no freedom as long as we remain bound by our self-centered perspective and blind to the impact each of us has on the world around us. This world, of which we are all temporary tenants, challenges us like never before. We are challenged to find hope. We are challenged to find faith. We are challenged to find joy in life amidst despair and anxiety. May each of us find the wisdom and courage to reflect sincerely on our lives, to discover our true purpose, and to accomplish nothing less than the rotation of an entire world. This is grace. We are grace. Let's begin now. Don't let the ferry leave without you.

G. K., November 1, 2001

A Note to Mental Health Professionals: Naikan and Psychotherapy

The material in this book provides a stark contrast to the ideas, methods, and theories that would generally appear in works based on more traditional Western approaches to mental health. If your work involves counseling, please consider the implications of what you've read as you provide guidance to those who seek your help. If you have come to the end of this book and wish to incorporate some or all of what you've read into your work, you will find below some of the challenges you will face as you adapt, adjust, and redefine a path of mental health for your clients and yourself.

Naikan has been used successfully in Japan, Europe, and the United States to respond to what we would call clinical problems. Specifically, it has been used in the areas of alcoholism and drug addiction, marriage and family therapy, rehabilitation of criminals, the education of children with behavioral problems, and work situations requiring conflict resolution. I have also seen the dramatic effects of Naikan reflection on those struggling with depression, anxiety, and even procrastination. Naikan is a wonderful community-building tool, in the family, the workplace, or anywhere a group of people are trying to live together and provide mutual support. Applying Naikan as a counselor to any of these situations will require a shift to a new perspective. Following are six critical areas where you may need to shift from a traditional therapeutic framework to a Naikan-based framework:

1. *TRADITIONAL: Focus on Feelings*
   NAIKAN: Focus on Facts

Many methods of psychotherapy emphasize feelings. They play a prominent role in the counseling session and are often used as a measure of mental health and as a principal criterion for decision making. Naikan searches for facts. Regardless of how you felt when you received a hand-me-down bicycle on your birthday, the fact is you received a bicycle. Though you may have been angry at your wife for what she said to you in the car, the fact is she drove you to the subway station. One psychologist who did a week-long Naikan retreat struggled for the first several days, until she suddenly came to a realization: "This is about what actually happened!"

It's not that Naikan denies the value of our emotions. It's just that we often become so preoccupied with our feelings that we fail to see the actual facts of the situation. Naikan gives us a clearer picture of the conduct of others on our behalf (question 1) and our own conduct toward others (questions 2 and 3). We have an opportunity to observe our life without the tint or discoloration of our fluctuating feelings. We try to see reality-as-it-is.

*2. TRADITIONAL: **Revisit How You've Been Hurt and Mistreated in the Past***
*NAIKAN: **Revisit How You've Been Cared for and Supported in the Past***

Many approaches to psychotherapy are founded on the unstated assumption that there is value and healing power in revisiting the pain and hurt we experienced in the past. The application of the term "victim" has expanded geometrically. The challenges and difficulties we've faced are redefined as trauma. The idea is that we must somehow revisit those traumas, get in touch with our feelings (for example, anger), and purge ourselves of those feelings to be healed. Yet there is little evidence to suggest that this theory is valid and much evidence to suggest that it is incorrect. One study of Holocaust survivors, cited in Terrence Des Pres's book *The Survivor,* points out "the magnificent ability of human beings to rebuild shattered lives, careers, and families, even as they wrestle with the bitterest of memories." Anton Antonovsky, after studying concentration camp survivors, writes, "a not inconsiderable number of concentration camp survivors were found to be well adapted. . . . What has given these women the strength, despite their experiences, to maintain what would seem to be the capacity not only to function well, but even to be happy?" Similar conclusions have been made about hostages. Reexperiencing our painful memories does not seem to get us anywhere except to a place with more pain.

Naikan offers the opposite prescription: let's revisit the many ways we were loved and cared for by others. But why should we do this? One reason is that it provides realistic context for our more difficult experiences. There is no attempt to deny that we experienced pain, but rather we try to view that pain in the larger context of the love and care others gave us. In several cases I have seen people who were sexually abused as children come to terms with their experiences as they saw all the care they received as a child. The care and love received were just as real as the abuse. Indeed, most of the time, if I just stop and reflect on my life *right now,* I see I am being supported in an infinite number of ways, from the chair I am sitting in to the air I am breathing. Any effort to seek the truth about our past must attempt to paint an accurate picture that includes everything, not just the pain.

3. TRADITIONAL: *The Therapist Validates the Client's Experience* NAIKAN: *The Therapist Helps the Client Understand the Experience of Others*

It is common for the therapist to begin by trying to understand and validate the client's experience. In extreme cases, therapists may be so concerned with confirming the client's experience that they discard any concern for the truth. Suppose I am bald but I am talking incessantly about how people admire my beautiful curly hair. If I am interested in learning the truth about my life, I don't need someone sitting across from me sympathetically agreeing with me. I need someone who will put a mirror in front of my face and say, "Look! You don't have any hair." Then I will learn something valuable about myself. Of course, most of us want to be understood by others. But a path with more integrity is to understand ourselves and to understand others. Haya Akegarasu, a Buddhist priest, said, "To understand oneself, to understand others—this ability belongs to us. When we understand ourselves and others we cannot help but open up a new road to our lives. But whether other people understand us or not—that can't be helped, that depends on other people." So perhaps a legitimate role for the therapist is to help the client understand others.

Naikan asks us to understand others by asking the third question: "What troubles and difficulties have I caused others?" To answer this question, we must put ourselves in someone else's shoes. What is it like for my wife to be married to me? What is it like for my colleague to work with me? If we can sincerely reflect on these questions, we can begin to understand the other person. And it is often such reflection that provides us with a new perspective on a situation. We are accustomed to seeing everything from our own self-centered perspective. But now, through self-reflection, we have a new lens with which to see things from the other person's perspective. Through our self-reflection we can begin to see into the heart of another human being, and this is the foundation for understanding and compassion toward others.

4. *TRADITIONAL:* **Blame Others for Your Problems**
   NAIKAN: **Take Responsibility for Your Own Conduct and the Problems You Cause Others**

It is refreshing to find someone who makes a mistake and then says, "I'm sorry. I made a mistake." If I meet someone who does that, I immediately consider him to be my teacher. Too often we make a mistake and blame someone else for it. It is also common, nowadays, to excuse our mistakes by blaming our faulty brain chemistry. Often when people undergo psychotherapy, they begin by blaming other people for their problems. But if the therapist simply allows this to continue, that is the biggest problem. Since we can't control other people, if they are the source of our problems, then we are doomed to a life of anger, resentment, disappointment, and frustration. A more meaningful approach for a counselor would be to help the client take responsibility for his own actions, particularly those that have been self-centered and caused difficulty for others. Of course, if our attention is always on how other people are causing us problems, we will never have any time to examine our own conduct and take responsibility for the way we have treated others.

Naikan challenges us to look honestly at our conduct and take responsibility for our actions, particularly those actions that have been a source of inconvenience, difficulty, or suffering for others. This is not necessarily easy to do. The therapist can point us in the right direction and gently help us get back on track when we find ourselves mired in blaming and judging others.

5. TRADITIONAL: *The Therapist Provides Analysis and Interpretation of the Client's Experience*
NAIKAN: *The Therapist Provides a Structured Framework for the Client's Self-Reflection*

In Western psychotherapy, the therapist commonly plays the role of analyst and interpreter. Dreams are dissected and given meaning. Feelings are excavated and purged. The absence of cooperation is redefined as resistance. All in all, the therapist plays a prominent role in the client's pursuit of new insight or understanding.

Insight and understanding are also important in Naikan, but the role of the therapist is quite different. She initially teaches the client this method of self-reflection and confirms its value through her personal commitment to self-reflection in her own life. Subsequently she provides structure and guidance by offering suggestions about whom to reflect on and for what period of time. She listens attentively to the client as he shares his reflection and generally offers little or no comment about what he has reflected on. Her authority, power, and expertise are not asserted because the underlying assumption is that any insight, understanding, or change in perspective comes from the client's self-reflection, not from her analysis or interpretation.

In some respects the Naikan therapist is like a research director for the investigation the client is doing about how he has lived. From her personal experience, she is familiar with some of the traps and pitfalls of the process; but she primarily watches with curiosity as the process unfolds and allows the researcher to draw his own conclusions.

6. TRADITIONAL: *Therapy Helps the Client Increase Self-Esteem* NAIKAN: *Therapy Helps the Client Increase Appreciation for Life*

One of the most common questions about Naikan is whether it is likely to reduce a person's self-esteem. It's a logical question since we may conclude that we have received more than we have given and also become acutely aware of the troubles we have caused other people. We may feel that we haven't done enough, or even feel guilty, which could be a real blow to our self-esteem.

In fact, Naikan does not address the issue of self-esteem at all, at least not directly. Instead, two other issues are given prominence:

the importance of having an accurate self-image and the need to appreciate the world around us.

If we wish to see the truth about our life, then truth must be given greater value than feeling good about ourselves. The Naikan therapist is there to help the client search for truth, and the image we have of ourselves should be an accurate reflection of the life we are living. If I have been of great service to others, if I have given my time, money, and attention in helping others, then those facts should be reflected in my self-image, not because they make me feel good but because they are facts. But if I have harmed others, deceived others, or made choices that were self-centered, then those are also facts that should be reflected in my self-image.

One of the outcomes of Naikan self-reflection is that we come away with a more accurate self-image. We attribute many emotional and psychological disorders to underestimating ourselves, but I would argue that, for most of us, our problem is that we overestimate ourselves. C. S. Lewis pointed this out insightfully when he said,

> We imply, and often believe, that habitual vices are exceptional single acts, and make the opposite mistake about our virtues— like the bad tennis player who calls his normal form his 'bad days' and mistakes his rare successes for his normal.

Finally, Naikan offers something much more important than self-esteem, which is an appreciation of the world around us. As the Naikan therapist helps redirect our attention to the world around us, we may come to see the many blessings that often go unnoticed. As we are humbled by awareness of our own limitations, we are more and more awed by the constancy, reliability, and sacredness of all the people and things that support our daily existence.

* * *

For the therapist who wishes to utilize Naikan in psychotherapy, her first task will be to utilize this method of self-reflection in her own life. In a mental health system that too often emphasizes techniques, Naikan is most effective when it is simply a natural extension of the therapist's approach to life. The therapist's ability to apply Naikan depends on her personal experience with it. Her usefulness as a guide down the path of self-reflection will be based on her commitment to making self-reflection an ongoing part of her own life. Formal training and retreats are available, and provide a strong foundation, but there is no substitute for ongoing practice. And for those of you who are in therapy or considering it, I encourage you to question the assumptions underlying the path you are being offered. Though some mental health professionals would lead us to believe that psychology is a science, it is much more a philosophy. Choose your philosophy consciously. Make sure your psychotherapy reflects your own personal values of how you wish to live your life. If your spiritual or religious traditions are important to you, make sure therapy supports, rather than distracts you from, those principles.

Moment by moment our life unfolds. There is great wisdom in observing how that happens. A wise path leads us in the direction of reality. How else can we find our way home?

Notes and Bibliography

NOTES AND CREDITS

Text notes are referenced by page number.

49 Shunryu Suzuki Roshi, from *Zen Mind, Beginner's Mind,* ed. Trudy Dixon (New York: Weatherhill, 1970), p. 118.

53 Kosho Uchiyama Roshi, from Shundo Aoyama, *Zen Seeds: Reflections of a Female Priest*, trans. Patricia Daien Bennage (Tokyo: Kosei, 1990), p. 23.

58 This essay was inspired by Albert Schweitzer's "Double Sermon on Gratitude: Fugal Theme and Counter Theme," preached by Dr. Schweitzer in 1919 in Strasbourg's Saint Nicolai Church.

73 David Dunn is the pen name of Robert R. Updegraff, who died in 1977. His son, Norman C. Updegraff, now publishes the most recent addition of this delightful book, entitled *Try Giving Yourself Away*. He can be contacted at Updegraff Press, 2564 Cherosen Road, Lousville, KY 40205.

86 Abbot John, from *The Wisdom of the Desert: Sayings from the Desert Fathers of the Fourth Century*, trans. Thomas Merton (New York: New Directions, 1960), p. 71.

95 Shundo Aoyama, from *Zen Seeds*, pp. 64–65.

114 Lewis Thomas, from *The Lives of a Cell: Notes of a Biology Watcher* (New York: Bantam Books, 1974), p. 2.

117 Lewis Thomas, from *The Lives of a Cell,* p. 86.

124 Shundo Aoyama, from *Zen Seeds*, p. 52.

131 Manshi Kiyozawa, from *December Fan,* trans. Nobuo Haneda (Kyoto: Higashi Honganji, 1984).

132 Thomas Merton, from *Love and Living.* New York: Bantam Books, 1965, p. 30.

135 Rumi, from *We Are Three*, trans. Coleman Barks (Athens, Ga.: Maypop Books, 1987).

144 Testimony excerpted from "Naikan for Those with Marriage Difficulties: A Case Study." Presented at the First International Naikan Congress, 1991, Tokyo, Japan.

145 Charlotte Joko Beck, from *Everyday Zen; Love and Work*, ed. Steve Smith (San Francisco: Harper San Francisco, 1989), p. 89.

151 Seikan Hasegawa Roshi, from *Essays on Marriage* (Arlington, Va.: Great Ocean Publishers, 1977), p. 48.

159 Pierre D'Amours, from "Naikan Diary," in *Flowing Bridges, Quiet Waters: Japanese Psychotherapies, Morita and Naikan,* ed. David K. Reynolds (Albany: SUNY Press, 1989), p. 129.

187 Albert Schweitzer, from *Albert Schweitzer: An Anthology*, ed. Charles R. Joy (Boston: Beacon Press, 1947), p. 95.

NAIKAN-RELATED RESOURCES

Green, Ron, and Gregg Krech. "Mirror of Buddha: The Contemplative Practice of Naikan." In *The Complete Guide to Buddhist America,* edited by Don Morreale, pp. 331–33. Boston: Shambhala, 1998.

Krech, Gregg. *Naikan: Hidden Gifts Revealed*. Middlebury, Vt.: Tōdō Institute, 1990. Audiotape.

———. *Naikan: The Practice of Attention and Reflection*. Middlebury, Vt.: TōDō Institute, 1995.

———. *A Natural Approach to Mental Wellness*. Middlebury, Vt.: TōDō Institute, 2000.

Kusano, Makoto. "Naikan Therapy for Alcohol Dependency: Its Mechanism of Action." *Constructive Living Quarterly* 2, no. 1 (spring 1994).

Reynolds, David K. *A Handbook for Constructive Living*. New York: William Morrow, 1995.

———, ed. *Flowing Bridges, Quiet Waters: Japanese Psychotherapies, Morita and Naikan*. Albany: SUNY Press, 1989.

———. *Naikan Psychotherapy: Meditation for Self-Development*. Chicago: University of Chicago Press, 1983.

———, ed. *Plunging through the Clouds: Constructive Living Currents*. Albany: SUNY Press, 1993.

———. *The Quiet Therapies: Japanese Pathways to Personal Growth*. Honolulu: University of Hawaii Press, 1980.

Takemoto, Takahiro. "Naikan and Alcohol Dependence: A Case Study." *Constructive Living Quarterly* 2, no. 1 (spring 1994).

Yoshimoto, Ishin. *Naikanho e no go-annai* (A guide to Naikan). Nara, Japan: Naikan Training Center, 1973.

RECOMMENDED READING

Akegarasu, Haya. *Shout of Buddha: Writings of Haya Akegarasu*. Translated by Gyoko Saito and Joan Sweany. Chicago: Orchid Press, 1977.

Aoyama, Shundo. *Zen Seeds: Reflections of a Female Priest*. Translated by Patricia Daien Bennage. Tokyo: Kosei, 1990.

Beck, Charlotte Joko. *Everyday Zen: Love and Work.* Edited by Steve Smith. San Francisco: Harper San Francisco, 1989.

Dunn, David. *Try Giving Yourself Away.* Louisville, Ky.: The Updegraff Press, 1970.

Haguri, Gyodo. *The Awareness of Self.* Kyoto: General Printing, 1967.

Hasegawa, Seikan. *Essays on Marriage.* Arlington, Va.: Great Ocean Publishers, 1977.

Hyde, Lewis. *The Gift: Imagination and the Erotic Life of Property.* New York: Vintage Books, 1983.

Kiyozawa, Manshi. *December Fan.* Kyoto: Higashi Honganji, 1984.

Krech, Gregg, and Linda Anderson. *A Finger Pointing to the Moon: A Workbook for Establishing Direction and Focus in Daily Life.* Middlebury, Vt.: TōDō Institute, 1996.

Kubose, Gyomay M. *The Center Within.* Union City, Calif.: Heian International, 1986.

Lemisch, Jesse L. *Benjamin Franklin: The Autobiography and Other Writings.* New York: Signet, 1961.

Lewis, C. S. *The Problem of Pain.* New York: Macmillan, 1962.

Merton, Thomas. *Love and Living.* New York: Bantam Books, 1965.

———, trans. *The Wisdom of the Desert: Sayings from the Desert Fathers of the Fourth Century.* New York: New Directions, 1960.

Millman, Dan. *The Laws of Spirit: Simple, Powerful Truths for Making Life Work.* Tiburon, Calif.: H. J. Kramer, 1995.

Mowrer, O. H. *The Crisis in Psychiatry and Religion.* Princeton: Van Nostrand, 1961.

Murphy, Gardner, with Morton Leeds. *Outgrowing Self-Deception.* New York: Basic Books, 1975.

Reynolds, David K. *Playing Ball on Running Water: The Japanese Way to Building a Better Life*. New York: William Morrow, 1984.

Schweitzer, Albert. *Reverence for Life: An Anthology of Selected Writings*. Edited by Thomas Kiernan. New York: Philosophical Library, 1965.

Suzuki, D. T. *Japanese Spirituality*. Translated by Norman Waddell. New York: Greenwood Press, 1972.

———. *Shin Buddhism*. New York: Harper and Row, 1970.

Suzuki, Shunryu. *Zen Mind, Beginner's Mind*. Edited by Trudy Dixon. New York: Weatherhill, 1970.

Thich Nhat Hanh. *Peace Is Every Step: The Path of Mindfulness in Everyday Life*. Edited by Arnold Kotler. New York: Bantam Books, 1991.

Thomas, Lewis. *The Lives of a Cell: Notes of a Biology Watcher*. New York: Bantam Books, 1974.

Uchiyama, Kosho. *Opening the Hand of Thought: Approach to Zen*. New York: Arkana, 1993.

Unno, Taitetsu. *Gratitude: Its Source and Power*. San Francisco: Buddhist Churches of America, 1991.

———. *River of Fire, River of Water: An Introduction to the Pure Land Tradition*. New York: Doubleday, 1998.

Index

For further information on Naikan, as well as Morita Therapy, Constructive Living, Meaningful Life Therapy, and Working with Challenging Children, please contact:

The TōDō Institute
P.O. Box 874
Middlebury, Vermont 05753
(802) 453-4440
e-mail: naikaninfo@todoinstitute.com
www.todoinstitute.org

STONE
BRIDGE
PRESS

STONE BRIDGE PRESS, P.O. BOX 8208, BERKELEY, CA 94707
To comment on this book or to receive a free catalog of other books about Japan and Japanese culture, contact Stone Bridge Press at
sbp@stonebridge.com / 1-800-947-7271 / www.stonebridge.com